HOW TO F...

PRIVATE COMPANY

Starting up and running a private company

BRIAN GOLDSTEIN
FCA ATII

Published by
Jordan & Sons Limited
15 Pembroke Road, Bristol BS8 3BA

Copyright © 1985 Jordan & Sons Limited

Thirtieth edition 1985

British Library Cataloguing in Publication Data
Goldstein, Brian
How to form a private company: starting up and running
a private company.—30th ed.
1. New business enterprises—Great Britain 2. Private
companies—Great Britain
I. Title
658.1′144′0941   HD62.5

ISBN 0-85308-083-6

Typeset by Leaper & Gard Ltd
Printed in Great Britain at Jordan Print Services, Bristol

Foreword
by David Trippier MP

Parliamentary Under Secretary of State for Employment & Minister for Small Firms

In recent years successive governments have increasingly appreciated the role of small firms in our economy. Many of today's most successful companies started life as one-man or family businesses.

The years of recession have forced the commercial world to re-examine its values and become more cost-effective. Although this period has been a painful one, it has produced a slimmer and more competitive industrial sector. But as we all know, one of the less fortunate by-products of this slimming down process has been increasing unemployment. Large firms have shed staff on a major scale and the resultant social problems and waste of talent are something which we must now tackle as a major priority.

Small businesses offer the potential to absorb much of this pool of under-utilized talent. It is for this reason that I, as Minister for Small Firms, and my officials in the Small Firms Division have been transferred to the Department of Employment, now headed by Lord Young who has had much experience in stimulating the creation of jobs in his previous roles as Chairman of the Manpower Services Commission and, more recently, as Minister without Portfolio with responsibility for the Government's Enterprise Unit. We now have a strong team, of which I am proud to be part, which can really tackle the problems of unemployment and job creation. A major part of our strategy will be encouragement of small businesses to prosper and expand and we shall need to approach this in a number of ways.

First, we must see that small business managers have time to do what they are best at − running their business, free from unnecessary burdens and restraints. Our work on deregulation − making life easier for the business man − will continue.

Secondly, we need to ensure that managers have access to proper training in business skills. The Manpower Services Commission have done sterling work already in providing a wide variety of courses, available through a number of different learning techniques. The provision of training is a vital part of our efforts to help the small business man and will continue.

Thirdly, we have to provide timely and expert advice to the small business manager. The Small Firms Service with its strong team of counsellors − all experienced business men − is available to small firms throughout the country. It can be contacted through Freefone Enterprise. In addition, there are now in many towns and cities local enterprise agencies which can also give advice and support to small businesses. These are funded to a great extent by the private sector and the Government welcomes the growing involvement of large and medium-sized firms in promoting strong local economies. While it will never be possible to eliminate all the risks involved in running a business, access to detailed and professional advice can help to avoid potential problems and take advantage of commercial opportunities.

As well as these initiatives, guidance is also needed on the main detailed aspects of setting up in business. Jordan & Sons Ltd, in this book, cover one particular aspect − forming a private company − and I am therefore particularly glad to have been invited to contribute a Foreword to this excellent publication.

DAVID TRIPPIER

Editor's Note

This is the 30th edition of this book which though modest in size provides invaluable information to anyone interested in starting a business. The book is an introduction to the formation of and the operation of a business through a limited company.

Although I have kept to the plan of the book as it has evolved over the years, the text of this edition has been completely revised and updated to take into account the major changes in the law affecting companies since the last edition. In addition Part IV of the book — 'Starting the Business of the Company' — goes further than any previous edition by examining the advice available to the proprietors of a private company, the type of finance available and where to find it and finally explains the importance of ensuring that the company is fully insured against the different misfortunes which a company may meet in the course of trading.

The law is stated as at 31 July 1985 and is based on the long awaited consolidation of the Companies Acts 1948 to 1983. The Companies Act 1985 received the royal assent on 11 March 1985 and its provisions came into force on 1 July 1985. References in the text to taxation include changes made by the Finance Act 1985.

I gratefully acknowledge the expert assistance of Miss Kim Lan Yap ACIS in reading and suggesting alterations to the text of this edition.

Brian Goldstein FCA, ATII

Contents

Introduction

This book is written primarily to assist those people who are thinking of starting up a business or are already running a small unincorporated business. It explains what a private company is and the advantages of trading through a private company. It then explains how to form and run a company. Finally, it looks at the government schemes, advisers, finance and insurance.

The statistics issued by the Department of Trade of the number of companies registered in England and Wales during the last ten years give a clear indication of the growth and importance of the private company in this country. These statistics also indicate the increasing awareness of the business community to the advantages of registering a private company when starting on a new enterprise.

Total number of companies on register at 1/1/85   952,912
Private companies 946,604   Public companies 6,308

New companies registered in England and Wales

1975	1976	1977	1978	1979	1980	1981	1982	1983	1984
43,428	53,819	52,872	60,611	62,958	66,104	68,941	82,955	91,470	92,932

The basic design of a limited company has not changed for over a century. Such tried and tested structure is support in itself for the status and prestige which a private company enjoys. An interesting point is that there are more incorporated companies in Great Britain than in all the remaining countries forming the European Economic Community.

Business men and women are recommended to take professional advice before converting a business to or forming a limited company. Having read this book you should be in a better position to make use of that advice.

Part I

Should I Form a Limited Company?

1.1 Types of Business Arrangement and Registration

Before starting to trade the owner(s) of a business must decide on the legal form it will take. The five more usual, legal forms of business are:

Sole Trader
As the sole trader or proprietor of a business you can trade either in your own name or a made-up name, the latter being called a business name. The regulations regarding the use of certain 'sensitive' words in a business name are dealt with in Appendix I. With the abolition in 1982 of the Registration of Business Names Act 1916 and the resultant closure of the Registry of Business Names there is now no central registry of persons or partnerships carrying on business in names other than personal names. This change has not been popular with banks, accountants, solicitors and other traders and has been a contributing factor in the considerable increase in the level of company formations since 1982.

The main disadvantage suffered by the entrepreneur who carries on business as a sole trader is that he accepts full responsibility for the business and its liabilities. In the eyes of the law the business and the proprietor are one and the same and in the event of financial problems all personal assets can be taken to pay creditors and can ultimately result in personal bankruptcy.

Partnership
When two or more persons carry on a business in common with a view to making a profit, a partnership exists. The financing and

running of the business is shared by the partners. Regulations regarding the names of partnerships are similar to those that apply to the sole trader as explained above. Trading as a partnership carries the same full responsibility for the business and its liabilities as with the sole trader. In fact the additional disadvantage is that each partner is liable for *all* the debts and obligations of the firm and although as between the partners themselves, each must contribute his proper share, a third party can if he likes look to any one of the partners for payment of the aggregate sum due to him and may enforce payment by legal action.

Limited Partnership

This type of partnership which must consist of one or more general partners and one or more limited partners was introduced under the Limited Partnership Act 1907. The general partners are liable for the debts and obligations of the firm, as in an ordinary partnership, but the limited partners are only liable to the extent of the sum contributed as capital at the time of entering the partnership. The limited partner must not take part in the management of the partnership business otherwise he becomes liable for all the debts of the firm incurred while he was taking part in the management as if he were a general partner. A limited partnership must be registered with the Registrar of Companies.

Unlimited Company

This is similar in structure and incorporation procedure to a limited company and has members and directors. It is subject to the same restrictions on choice of name and has to be registered with the Registrar of Companies. It can be registered with or without share capital and the rules and regulations governing its external and internal affairs are laid out in its memorandum and articles of association. It is not required to publish accounts with the Registrar of Companies, provided it is not (a) a subsidiary of one (or more) limited companies; (b) the holding company of a limited company; or (c) running a trading stamp scheme.

As is apparent from its name the main feature is that the liability of the members is unlimited and therefore the risks inherent in trading as a sole trader or partnership equally apply to this type of company. In addition an ex-member of an unlimited company in liquidation can be liable for debts incurred while he was a member if he had been a member within the year prior to the company going into liquidation.

Limited Company

This enjoys many advantages not enjoyed by the other types of business arrangement described above and they are explained in detail in the remainder of this book.

1.2 Different Types of Limited Company

Public Limited Companies

These are limited companies which can offer their shares or debentures for sale to the public. Many public limited companies (plc) are quoted on the Stock Exchange and their shares can be purchased and sold by members of the public through stockbrokers.

Being issued with its certificate of incorporation does not entitle the plc to commence trading or to exercise any of its borrowing powers. It must also be issued with a certificate to commence trading by the Registrar of Companies. To apply for such a certificate the company must have an allotted share capital of not less than the authorized minimum (at present £50,000)* one-quarter of which nominal value (and the whole of any premium) must be paid up.

The name of such a company must end with the words 'public limited company' or 'plc'.

Companies Limited by Guarantee

These are usually non-profit making companies formed for charitable, religious, educational, sporting or similar objectives. They do

---

* These requirements do not apply to private companies.

not have a share capital and each member undertakes to contribute a specified sum (usually £1) towards the liabilities of the company in the event of its being wound up. Being registered as a guarantee company is ideal for associations, societies and clubs.

The advantages enjoyed of being a registered company with separate legal identity make it more convenient for the purchasing or leasing of premises, the employment of staff, and for entering into contracts. Probably the most common type of guarantee company is that formed to manage a block of flats and to deal with the upkeep thereof including the maintenance of gardens, lifts, paths and common parts. In general a guarantee company is appropriate where the pursuit of profit is not the main object and is a convenient form of incorporation for a small or large group of persons with a common interest.

Private Companies

The total number of companies on the official register of companies as at 1 January 1985 was 952,912 of which over 99 per cent were private companies. Of the companies registered in 1984 85 per cent had a nominal share capital of £5,000 or under.

Unlike the position in many other countries, the structure of a small private company and the law which governs its operation are similar to that of and applicable to the largest and most reputable quoted public company. The main distinction between public and private companies is that the latter are prohibited from inviting the public to subscribe for any of their shares or debentures. Another clause which is normally inserted in the articles of association of a private company enables the directors to decline to register any transfer of shares to a person of whom they do not approve, without giving any reason for their refusal.*

In Parts II and III we shall be examining in detail the legal structure of a private company and the legal requirements before and after incorporation.

---

* Prior to the Companies Act 1980 this was a compulsory provision.

1.3 Advantages of Trading as a Limited Company

Numerous advantages are derived from running a business as a private company. These are listed below for ease of reference, the first six of which are the principal advantages and are dealt with in detail in 1.4–1.9 at pages 8 to 15.

- A private company is a separate legal entity.

- The liability of the members is limited.

- The name of your company is protected against duplication.

- Advantages are available when borrowing money.

- Continuity of existence of the company.

- In certain circumstances there are taxation advantages. Advice from a professionally qualified accountant or solicitor is recommended before incorporation.

- The respective interests and responsibilities of the persons engaged in the business are clearly defined including the management responsibilities of the directors of the company.

- There are more generous pension possibilities for the directors of a company than there are for the sole trader where contributions are limited to 17.5 per cent of net relevant earnings (see *Pensions* at p. 15 below).

- The appointment, retirement or removal of directors are effected in a simple manner.

- Employees may, with adequate safeguards, be given an opportunity of acquiring shares in the company related to their positions and responsibilities. Equally it is relatively simple to introduce new outside shareholders to the Company.

- For non-resident persons a United Kingdom private company is a cost-effective tax haven without the stigma and excessive annual cost, attached to companies formed in the well-known low tax areas. Provided these companies are managed and controlled from outside the UK and do not trade in the UK no UK corporation tax is payable on their profits. In addition the company must have no place of business in the UK. These companies are known as non-resident UK companies.

1.4 Separate Identity

When a company is incorporated a new and separate legal entity is created which is apart from the members comprising it. It can purchase, sell, rent and lease premises and property; it can carry on a business which is quite separate and distinct from any other business the owner, members or directors of the company may have; it can sue and be sued; it can enter into and rescind contracts. All these can be done by the company quite independently of the activities of its members.

1.5 Limited Liability

Unquestionably the main and most important advantage of a private company is the protection afforded by limited liability. The members or shareholders have no liability to contribute to debts of the company beyond any amount unpaid on any shares issued to them. However in most private companies shares are issued as 'fully paid' which means that if things go wrong shareholders will lose the value of their shares and possibly any loans they have made to the company but nothing more. Obviously if they have had to guarantee a bank overdraft or the rent on the company's premises then they will be liable for these debts in the event of liquidation caused by the insolvency of the company.

A situation where the protection of limited liability is of

particular importance is the case of a sole trader who has two separate businesses. In the event of one of the businesses becoming insolvent and ceasing to trade the creditors of that business have a claim against all the sole trader's assets including his successful solvent firm. If however the insolvent firm had been trading as a private company then the creditors of that company would not normally have a claim against the assets of the other firm whether operated as a sole trader or as a separate limited company.

The Companies Acts are not immune from criminal abuse and opportunities have always existed for defrauding the unwary. However it has to be said that the minute percentage of fraud is a small price to pay compared with the benefit derived by the community as a whole from the increased entrepreneurial activity prompted by the limited liability afforded to persons contemplating new businesses. Most of our major public quoted companies would never have started but for the facilities for obtaining capital and the opportunities for getting started facilitated by the Companies Acts.

The protection of limited liability does not extend to 'fraudulent trading'. Directors of companies have a duty not to knowingly incur debts they have reason to believe the company cannot and is unlikely to be able to repay. If they do and the company's creditors lose their money the directors and anyone else who may have been involved could personally face allegations of fraudulent trading. In those circumstances the court can make those involved personally liable without limit. This situation has always existed but the police and courts have found it very difficult to establish guilt.*

1.6 Protection of Company Name

The provisions of the Companies Act 1985 give protection against the duplication of company names by stating that the Registrar shall not register a company with the name of a company already

* See footnote to page 28.

9

on the index of company names kept by him.

The Department of Trade also has powers under section 28 of the Companies Act 1985 to direct any company to change its name within twelve months of incorporation if it has been registered in a name which is the same as or 'too like' a name already on the index.*

No such protection against duplication of name is afforded to persons carrying on business as a sole trader or partnership. If a firm ascertains that its name is being used by another commercial enterprise its only recourse is to consider a 'passing off' action by which it may be able to obtain damages and an order from the court stopping the 'theft' of the goodwill in its name. However this type of action can be very expensive, protracted and extremely difficult to prove.

The only other protection available with regard to names is that available under the Trade Marks Act 1938 for goods and products. Well-known trade marks such as Persil, Gillette, Heinz and TyPhoo are protected against duplication by registration under this Act. These goods are readily distinguished by the purchasing public from similar goods of other traders. Registration of a trade mark confers a statutory monopoly in the use of that mark in relation to the goods for which it is registered, and the registered owner has the right to sue in the courts for infringement of his mark.

The registration of a trade mark is quite separate and distinct from the registration of a limited company. In 2.1 (page 17), 'Choosing a Company Name' further reference is made to company names and trade marks.

1.7 Borrowing Advantages

Most new businesses need to borrow money in order to expand or to trade efficiently and profitably. A private company is normally

* See Appendix ID.

in an advantageous position to borrow money because several unique provisions prevail in its structure to facilitate this:

(1) *Ordinary Shares*

These can be issued to a prospective supplier of finance to provide permanent capital for the company. However these will normally carry voting rights and a share of profits.*

(2) *Preference Shares*

These also provide permanent capital but are often issued subject to redemption after a particular period or upon the happening of a specific event. These usually carry a fixed rate of dividend and provided this is paid on time the holder thereof will not normally have the right to attend and vote at any meetings of the company.

The word 'preference' relates to the right of the preferential shareholder to be paid interest in priority to the payment of dividends to other classes of shareholder. It also relates to preferential repayment of share capital in priority to repayment to other classes of shareholder in the event of the winding up of the company.

(3) *Debentures*

In the same way as ordinary and preference shares do, debentures provide permanent capital. These are issued carrying a fixed rate of interest and often either a fixed charge or a floating charge on some or all of the assets of the company. Even if issued carrying no charge on the assets (a simple or 'naked' debenture) debentures nevertheless enjoy preference with regard to payment of interest and repayment of capital in the event of the company being wound up.

(4) *Loans and Bank Overdrafts*

These are secured by a 'floating charge'. The floating charge 'floats' or 'hovers' over all or some of the assets of the company as they exist or change from time to time. Stock-in-trade, book debts,

* See 4.11, page 64 and 4.16, page 68.

furniture, equipment, machinery, goodwill and other non-specific assets may be used as security through a floating charge and, most importantly, while the subject of the charge, may be freely dealt with by the company in the ordinary course of its business. The only time that the free use of these assets ceases is if the company fails to pay interest or repay capital or commits some other breach of the provisions contained in the loan agreement. The charge then becomes fixed and from that date the company can no longer deal with the assets.

Directors of a private company formed to undertake a new enterprise would probably be required by their bankers to support a floating charge with personal guarantees. However when the business has begun to establish itself the floating charge enlarges the borrowing capacity of the business but only when it is operated as a limited company.

(5) *Business Expansion Scheme*
We deal with this scheme in 4.15 (page 68) as a source of raising capital. Basically the Government have made it tax advantageous for investors under the Business Expansion Scheme (BES) to invest their money in new or existing trading limited companies based in the UK. The investor is granted tax relief at his top rate of tax on the amount invested and the company obtains much needed finance. There are several venture capital companies who specialise in attracting this type of venture capital.

1.8 Continuity of Existence

As previously mentioned when a private company is formed a new separate legal entity or 'person' is created which is distinct from the individuals who compose it. On the death of a member his shares change hands, but the company goes on; whereas a partnership has no existence apart from the partners themselves, and in the absence of agreement to the contrary is dissolved upon the death of a partner.

A company once formed has everlasting life; the directors and members may change but the company lives on.

Being an artificial creation a company can only cease to exist on the happening of either of two events:

(a) The winding up or liquidation of the company.*
(b) The dissolution of the company by the Registrar of Companies under sections 652/3 of the Companies Act 1985.*

1.9 Taxation

(1) *Sole Traders*
Sole traders pay income tax on the profits of their business which are calculated after deducting expenses and capital allowances. The income tax payable is on a graduated scale, after personal allowances have been deducted. The rates of income tax start at 30 per cent at the lowest level of income (up to £16,200) and at progressive rates up to 60 per cent at the highest level of income (over £40,200) for the tax year 1985/86.

Directors, who in most small companies are the owners of the company, are taxed on their remuneration under PAYE on the same income tax graduated scale explained above.

Private companies pay corporation tax on the profits calculated after deducting expenses, directors' remuneration and capital allowances. The rate of corporation tax for the financial year 1984 (the year ending 31 March 1985 will be 45 per cent). However if a private company's profits are below £100,000 the corporation tax is 30 per cent (the small companies rate). There is a marginal relief where profits are between £100,000 and £500,000.

Set out below is an example of how at certain levels of

* See 3.20, pages 53 and 54, on winding up.

income the sole trader may reduce tax payable by forming and trading as a private company. As the calculations do not take into account individual circumstances of the company, its shareholders and directors, readers are recommended to consult their own professional advisers before proceeding with the formation of a company for taxation mitigation purposes.

Example
For the purpose of this example we assume that a business earned assessable profits after expenses and capital allowances for 1985/86 of £40,000. Additionally the owner of the business had other income equal to his personal allowances for tax purposes.

Tax payable if business operated by a sole trader:

		£
1st	£16,200 @ 30% tax	4,860
next	£ 3,000 @ 40% tax	1,200
next	£ 5,200 @ 45% tax	2,340
next	£ 7,900 @ 50% tax	3,950
remaining	£ 7,700 @ 55% tax	4,235
	£40,000	16,585

Less: tax relief on national insurance contributions	157
	16,428

Tax payable if business operated by a private company and the owner/director of the company draws remuneration of £5,400 and the company declares and pays a dividend of £10,000.*

---

* For the purposes of this example the imputation system of corporation tax which affects the date of payment of the tax but not the amount has been ignored (see 3.16(2), page 49).

	£
Profits of company	40,000
Less director's remuneration	5,400
Net profit subject to corporation tax	34,600

	£
Corporation tax @ 30%	10,380
Income tax on remuneration @ 30%	1,620
	12,000

Ignoring any other personal circumstances or considerations it can be seen that in the year in question there is a saving of tax of £4,428.

Against this must be set the additional national insurance contributions (less tax thereon) of £12.

(2) *Pensions*

Private companies and their controlling directors can gain considerable tax advantages by paying pension contributions out of profits into a life insurance company's pension scheme to provide funds from which pensions can be paid upon retirement. The amounts that can be allocated from profits are more generous than the 17.5 per cent of net relevant earnings which sole traders can contribute to a pension scheme.

In addition self-administered pension schemes are available whereby the amounts paid into the pension fund are fully allowable for corporation tax purposes and the amounts contributed go into a fund:

(a) which pays no tax on income or capital gains;
(b) whose investments are administered by the members of the scheme;
(c) which can be used to purchase the premises from which the company trades;
(d) which can lend money to the private company to ease cash flow; and
(e) where the contributions into the fund can be varied from year to year to fit in with the company's cash flow.

15

Part II
How to Form a Private Limited Company

Forming a limited company in the UK is probably simpler and less expensive than in any of the other major countries in the world. This part of the book explains in some detail what is a very technical subject.

2.1 Choosing a Company Name

Obviously depending upon the type of business the private company is to carry on a lot of thought will go into the choice of name. Where a company is merely to hold one property or undertake one transaction the name is not important and a ready-made company which most company registration agents stock will normally suffice. Ready-made companies are not, as is generally thought, companies which have ceased trading but are, in fact, newly incorporated companies which have not commenced trading and therefore have no assets or liabilities. They are registered with a minimum share capital (normally £100), for a particular type of business and for the sole purpose of being sold for immediate trading by the purchasers.

Solicitors, accountants and chartered secretaries will normally be able to obtain ready-made companies and they usually acquire these from a company registration agent* who forms these with standard memorandum and articles of association settled by barristers or solicitors specializing in company law. Purchasers of ready-made companies are recommended to only use registration agents who are members of the Association of Company Regis-

* See Appendix III.

17

tration Agents Ltd.

Some people tend to select a name which is wholly descriptive of their business whereas others use either a personal name or one which is both distinctive and descriptive of the business. This is very much a matter of personal choice but generally the shorter a name the more likely customers and prospective customers will remember it, e.g. Tesco Plc. Further evidence of this is the number of companies which are better known by the abbreviation of their name, e.g. ICI (Imperial Chemical Industries Plc) and BP (British Petroleum Plc). With approximately 950,000 limited companies on the live index of names kept by the Registrar of Companies the chances of finding a short name which is unique are very remote.

The Registrar of Companies no longer provides the free service of checking on the availability or advisability of new company names prior to the lodging of registration documents. Accordingly a person wishing to form a company must arrange this himself. This can be done at the offices of the Registrar of Companies in Cardiff and Edinburgh or at Companies House, London. Alternatively solicitors, accountants, chartered secretaries, company registration agents or some chambers of commerce provide this service for a small fee.

The freedom of choice in the selection of a company name is restricted in several ways. The name:

(a) Must not be the name of another company. For the purpose of deciding whether two names are the same such words as 'the', 'company', 'and company' and other abbreviations or Welsh equivalents are ignored. So are capital letters and punctuation.

(b) Must not include certain 'sensitive' words and expressions without the consent of the Secretary of State or some other relevant person or body. The use of certain words is controlled by other statutes. For example under section 36 of the Banking Act 1979 only a person authorized under that section is permitted to use a name which may 'reasonably be understood to indicate that he is a bank or banker or carrying on a banking business'. A list of these 'sensitive'

18

words and expressions is set out in Appendix I A, B and C of this book.

(c) Must not give the impression that the company is connected in any way with HM Government or with any local authority in England, Wales or Scotland.

(d) Must not include except at the end of the name, the words 'Limited', 'Unlimited', 'Public Limited Company' or their abbreviations or Welsh equivalents.

(e) Must not be offensive or its use must not constitute a criminal offence.

(f) Must have 'Limited' (or the Welsh equivalent 'Cyfyngedig') as the last word in its name unless exempted from such requirement.

There are circumstances where the Secretary of State has the power to direct a company to change its name. These are:

(a) If a company is registered with a name which is the same as or 'too like' a name already appearing on the index.* He can do this within 12 months of incorporation of a new private company. This provision allows aggrieved companies to make representations to the Secretary of State to persuade him to exercise this power.

(b) If within five years of the date of registration of a name he believes that misleading information was provided for the purposes of registration.

(c) If at any time the name by which it is registered 'gives so misleading an indication of the nature of its activities as to be likely to cause harm to the public'.

Another possible problem which should be checked before registering a new company name, to prevent subsequent difficulties, is that relating to trade marks. If the name is applied to goods its use may infringe the rights of the proprietor of an existing trade mark. This can be checked at the Trade Marks Registry in the

* See Appendix ID.

appropriate classes of goods for the trade to be carried on by the new private company. The main problem arises with invented or made-up names rather than a proper name or word in general use. Even though trade marks can only be registered in respect of goods, the common-law rights of the user of an unregistered name can also relate to services as well as goods. The position regarding unregistered names is difficult to check but an aggrieved owner of such a name would find it much more difficult to prove there has been an infringement and in addition would have to prove the public had been confused.

Finally two things are to be remembered with the name of your company:

(a) That you must be consistent in all documents presented for registration and on company stationery throughout the life of the company, e.g. If 'First Sausage and Meat Company Ltd' is a registered limited company the company must not add, to or abbreviate it so that it reads: *The first sausage & meat Co.* Ltd. This contains six mistakes 'The' has been added, 'and' and 'company' have been abbreviated to '&' and 'Co.' and the capital letters 'F', 'S' and 'M' have been printed in lower case.

(b) That until the Registrar of Companies issues the certificate of incorporation it is inadvisable to incur expenditure on the printing of letterheads and other stationery.

2.2 Documents to Be Completed

Having agreed upon the name of the proposed company we must now consider the documents that have to be completed and lodged with the Registrar of Companies so that he will attend to the incorporation of the company. These are as follows:

● Memorandum of association.

● Articles of association.

- Statement of particulars of first director(s) and secretary and situation of first registered office (Form G10*). This statement must also contain a signed consent by the persons named as first director(s) and secretary that they agree to act in their respective capacities and must be signed and dated at the foot of the form by a director or secretary prior to lodging.

- Statement of particulars of shares to be issued on incorporation (Form PUC1) which form must be signed and dated by a director or secretary prior to lodging.

- Declaration of compliance with the requirements of the Companies Act (Form G12). This may be made and signed either by a solicitor engaged in the formation or by a person named in the Form G10 as a director or secretary. This must be declared before a Commissioner for Oaths or Notary Public or Justice of the Peace or solicitor having the powers conferred on a Commissioner for Oaths and such person must also state the place where the declaration was made, sign and date the form.

The memorandum and articles of association must be signed by at least two subscribers. They must write opposite to their names the number of shares they agree to take. Usually only one is signed for, but any number a subscriber is prepared to pay for may be inserted. The full names and postal addresses of the subscribers must be given and their signatures must be attested by one or more witnesses, whose signature, full name and address are also required.

Minors should not be permitted to subscribe as they may repudiate the shares on or before attaining their majority. Other companies may subscribe to the memorandum and articles by having one of their directors or secretaries sign on their behalf. In such a situation it must be made clear that the signatory has signed for and on behalf of the corporate member.

* Form numbers were changed by the Companies Forms Regulations 1985.

In Appendix II to this book copies of the above mentioned forms and of the signed pages of the memorandum and articles of association are illustrated.

When these documents have been completed, signed and dated they may be lodged by post or by hand at the Companies Registry together with the appropriate capital duty (if any) at the rate of £1 per cent on the capital subscribed for and the official registration fee of £50. When accepted by the Registrar the documents are scrutinized and the proposed name checked. If the documents are correct he issues his certificate of incorporation which gives the date of signature and the registered number of the company. This procedure can take any time from two weeks upwards dependent on various factors including the volume of applications for new company registration. From the date of the issue of the certificate of incorporation the subscribers — together with others who may from time to time become members of the company — form a body corporate, capable of exercising all the functions of an incorporated company. In view of the importance of this date the promoters of the company must be careful not to enter into any binding contracts prior to that date otherwise they may be held personally responsible for and liable thereunder.

2.3 Memorandum of Association

The constitution of the company is set out in two documents: the memorandum of association and the articles of association. The memorandum lays down the company's powers and its relationship with the outside world and the articles regulate dealings between the company and its members, directors and other officers.

The memorandum of association must contain the following clauses:

(a) The name of the company, with 'Limited' or the abbreviation 'Ltd' as the last word.

(b) The situation of the registered office, i.e. whether it is in England, England and Wales, Wales or Scotland.

(c) The objects of the company.

(d) A statement that the liability of the members is limited.

(e) The amount of share capital the company is to be registered with, and its division into different classes of shares.

Clause 1: Name of the Company

This is covered in 2.1 (page 17). In this clause the full name of the company must be set out and if the registered office of the company (in clause 2) is to be in Wales the name of the company may be ended with the Welsh equivalent of limited (Cyfyngedig). Additionally in such a case the complete memorandum and articles may be filed in Welsh together with an English translation.

Clause 2: Situation of the Registered Office

This clause must state where the registered office is to be. There are four possibilities (a) England (b) England and Wales (c) Wales and (d) Scotland. The exact area in which the registered office will be sited, i.e. the town or county must not be specified. The wording must read 'The company's registered office is to be situated in England,' etc. Documents of companies whose registered office will be situated in Scotland must be lodged at Companies Registration Office in Edinburgh. These will be classified as Scottish companies.

Clause 3: Objects of the Company

This clause is invariably the longest and requires very careful consideration. The objects clause is divided into a number of sub-clauses of which the first will cover the main business of the company. It is important for this sub-clause to state clearly and comprehensively all the businesses and activities anticipated by the promoters. However as it is fairly simple to amend these by special resolution subsequent to incorporation, all is not lost if the original drafted objects are inadequate.

The second sub-clause is usually a 'mopping up' clause which covers any other business which in the opinion of the directors may be advantageously or conveniently carried on in conjunction with the main business of the company.

There then follow a series of sub-clauses which cover the general objects which most companies will need. These normally include the power to purchase, lease and sell property; to construct any buildings, plant and machinery; to borrow money; to mortgage or charge the undertaking, property and assets of the company; to acquire patents; to purchase shares in other companies; to issue shares and debentures; to invest money; to enter into partnership; to acquire businesses; to sell the undertaking of the company; to draw bills of exchange and negotiable instruments; to establish associations and clubs to benefit directors and employees; and to distribute property to members and to do all such other things as may be deemed incidental or conducive to the attainment of the main objects. This list is merely an abridged selection of the common general objects.

Since the European Communities Act of 1972 all transactions by the directors in the name of the company are binding against the company even if they are apparently not permitted by the memorandum of association. However the shareholders are not prevented from bringing an action against the directors for misfeasance.

Clause 4: Liability of Members
This must be worded 'the liability of the members is limited'. Which means that the liability of the members is limited to paying for the number of shares they have applied for and have been allotted. If they have paid for those shares in full then they have no further liability in the event of the company being liquidated.

Clause 5: Share Capital
This clause must state the capital, its division into class and number of shares, and the nominal value of each share usually £1. The shares may be divided into two or more classes, with different nominal values and rights attaching to each class. As previously explained the two main classes of share are 'ordinary' and 'preference'.

The classes of shares and the respective rights conferred on the holders may also be stated in this clause of the memorandum of association, but this is rarely done in practice as it is then more difficult to vary the rights at a later date. It is better to mention this in the articles so that any alteration or modification can then be effected by passing a special resolution.

Special Clauses in the Memorandum of Association
Although it is not usual practice to include other clauses in the memorandum of association occasionally this does happen. For the reasons given in the previous paragraph this procedure is not recommended unless the clauses are of a permanent nature.

2.4 Articles of Association

Every company must have articles of association regulating its internal affairs. These regulations govern the relationship between the company and its shareholders and the relationship of the shareholders between themselves.

A new Table A came into force on the 1 July 1985 and contains a model set of articles which is in the main satisfactory for private companies. Accordingly it is normal to adopt articles which incorporate Table A and any modifications required. This avoids the necessity of reproducing 118 regulations in the articles.

Because there are so many regulations it is possible to comment on only the more important provisions.

Classes of Shares
Where the capital of a company is divided into several classes of shares it is important to define the rights attaching to each class. Some shares may rank in priority to others, not only for dividend but, in the event of winding up, also repayment of original capital.* They may also carry greater voting power than other shares. The

* See 1.7, (2) Preference Shares, page 11.

articles may indicate the way in which the rights attaching to different classes of share may be altered, or new rights or classes of shares created. When the articles do not state otherwise this may be achieved by passing an ordinary resolution (Table A regulation 32).

Restrictions on Issue of Shares

The Companies Act 1985 (sections 89–96) gives existing members of limited companies a statutory right of pre-emption (the right of first refusal) over most new share issues. Accordingly any new shares to be issued must first be offered, on the proposed issue terms, to existing shareholders pro rata (in proportion) to their holding (at a specified date). Shareholders must be notified in writing and the offer must be open for at least 21 days. However private companies may specify in their articles of association that these statutory rights shall not apply and may give the directors discretion regarding share issues or incorporate other suitable regulations to comply with the original promoters' requirements. Where the authority to allot shares has been given to the directors, this must be renewed every five years.

Restriction on the Transfer of Shares

Although Table A, which is designed for both public and private companies, does not do so, it is usual for the articles of association of a private company to provide that the directors, in their absolute discretion and without having to give a reason, may decline to register any transfer of shares. Often the right of pre-emption, referred to above, is given to existing shareholders when a member wishes to sell his shares. Where this right is conferred the articles will contain elaborate provisions regarding the procedure to be followed, the time allowed to find members willing to purchase the shares, the method to be adopted in agreeing the price of the shares and the method of appointing an arbitrator when a price cannot be agreed.

Although it is relatively simple to change the articles of association after incorporation, it is wise to give the question of issue and transfer of shares a lot of thought before the company formation documents are filed at Companies House. In the normal husband and wife business situation there should be no major post-incorporation snags unless domestic problems arise, when it may not be possible for the two parties to agree on any necessary changes to the articles. Equally the same may apply where a dispute develops, after incorporation, between unconnected promoters of a company. The main matter to consider is whether the directors shall have the power to block transfers to children, husbands, wives and other relatives either during a shareholder's lifetime or on his or her death. There are arguments for and against such a power and much will depend upon the personal circumstances of the promoters.

Purchase of Its Own Shares

Since the Companies Act 1981 it has been possible for a private company to purchase its own shares provided specific authority for this is reserved in the articles of association. However regulation 35 of the new Table A permits this without need for specific authority and so a separate article is no longer required if Table A is adopted in the company's articles. Before actually taking any such action professional advice should be sought regarding the taxation implications of the company purchasing its own shares.

Number of and Appointment of Directors

The number of directors is normally specified in the articles by stating a minimum and maximum number. Table A regulation 64 provides that 'the number of directors shall not be subject to any maximum but shall be not less than two'. A private company may have only one director but such a sole director cannot also be secretary of the company. As it is necessary to file a statement naming the first directors with the registration documents it follows that the choice of officers is usually made by the subscribers. The articles of the company will normally determine the method of electing subsequent directors.

No general qualifications are needed to act as a company director although certain conditions do disqualify a person from so

27

acting. The main two conditions are bankruptcy and disqualification under the Companies Acts.*

The Companies Acts do not require directors to hold shares of the company they hold office in. However it is permissible to include an article which provides that a shareholding qualification is necessary.

It is not uncommon for one or more directors to be named as permanent directors in the articles in order to avoid the necessity of retirement by rotation. This method of achieving permanence is not recommended, but will be accomplished in one of two ways:

(a) By a separate agreement between the director and the company. Even this is vulnerable to an ordinary resolution being passed by the members to remove the director. If however the removal involves a breach of an agreement the director may be able to claim compensation or damages.

(b) Where the permanence is required for a director who is a member of the company his position can be protected by attaching enhanced voting rights to his shares so that in the event of a resolution to remove him being proposed his extra voting power would enable him to prevent the resolution from being passed.

Powers of Directors and Their Remuneration

The power to run a company is vested in the board of directors who will normally exercise this function through resolutions passed at duly convened board meetings. In practice, in larger companies, the board meets to discuss and formulate general policy and leaves the day to day decision making to a managing director and small committee of directors. This delegation of directors powers will be provided for in the articles. In the smaller company consisting of

* There are proposals in the Insolvency Bill now before Parliament which would if they became law in their present form (1) make directors in certain circumstances personally liable for some or all of a company's debts where it has traded wrongfully, (2) allow the court to make a disqualification order against a director of an insolvent company in certain circumstances.

two or three directors the legal requirements are the same but in practice decision making can be achieved on a daily basis by all directors.

In addition to providing that the business of the company shall be managed by the directors it is also usual to include a regulation stating that the directors may exercise all the powers of the company to borrow money, to mortgage its property and to issue securities. If required, it is possible to limit the total amount of debt the directors may incur on behalf of the company at any one time without the prior consent of the shareholders.

Directors remuneration and expenses need to be authorized in the articles. Table A provides for the payment of such remuneration as the company may by ordinary resolution determine. Table A also provides for the payment of all travelling, hotel and other expenses properly incurred by them in connection with their attendance at meetings of the directors or of the company. It is normally desirable from the director's point of view that he is employed under a service contract which covers his remuneration, bonuses or share of profits and reimbursement of expenses.

General Provisions

The remaining provisions of Table A or of a full set of articles deal with many items including a company's lien on every share for all moneys payable in respect of that share; making calls on members in respect of moneys payable on shares; forfeiture of shares where calls have not been paid; transmission of shares on the death of shareholders; alteration of share capital; general meetings, notice thereof and proceedings thereat; votes of members at meetings of the company; the appointment by directors of alternative directors; the disqualification and removal of directors; appointment of the company secretary; keeping of minutes of appointments of officers and of all proceedings of meetings; use of the company seal; declaration and payment of dividends; and winding up and indemnity of directors.

2.5 Duties and Fees Payable

An official fee of £50 is payable to the Registrar of Companies when lodging documents in respect of the formation of a company. The fee stamp is affixed on the memorandum of association. In addition capital duty is payable on the subscribed share capital which is determined by the value of the consideration payable by the subscribers on incorporation for the shares they agree to take up. This duty is payable when filing form PUC1 (statement of shares to be issued on incorporation) at the rate of £1 for every £100 of capital issued.

2.6 Incorporation

The company exists from the date that the Companies Registration Office issues the certificate of incorporation. This certificate is numbered, dated and signed by an authorized officer who certifies that the company name is this day incorporated under the Companies Act 1985 as a private company and that the company is limited. The number of the company cannot subsequently be changed and this remains the best way to identify a company where it has, subsequent to incorporation, changed its name.

2.7 Transfer of Existing Business to a Limited Company

This is normally accomplished by the proprietor/s of the business entering into an agreement for sale with the limited company whereby the company acquires the business in exchange for ordinary shares issued at par. All assets and liabilities are valued and taken over by the company. No capital gains tax will be chargeable on the transfer of the business where the total consideration is the issue of shares. The agreement for sale and Form PUC3 must be lodged with the Registrar of Companies. The agreement for sale must be stamped with 1 per cent *ad valorem* (according to the value) stamp duty on certain of the assets. No duty is payable on the agreement for sale where the total consideration does not exceed £30,000 and where the agreement contains a statement known as a 'Certificate of Value' certifying that 'the transaction hereby effected does not form part of a larger transaction or a series of transactions in respect of which the amount or value or aggregate amount or value of the consideration exceeds £30,000'.

Part III
Running Your New Company

Running a company is necessarily more complex than running an ordinary unincorporated firm. Company law imposes certain statutory duties as a small price for the benefits conferred on the private limited liability company. This part of the book sets out some of the requirements of the law which affect companies and their officers and also includes other useful information.

3.1 Registered Office

Every private company must have a registered office, to which all communications may be addressed and notices served. This need not be the main trading address of the company and is often the address of the company's accountants or solicitors. The registered office determines the tax district which will deal with the returns and tax matters of the company other than PAYE, which is usually covered by the collector of taxes local to the trading address or other address where the wages records are maintained.

3.2 Display of Company Name

Every private company is required to affix or paint its name on the outside of its registered office and every office, factory or place in which its business is carried on, in a conspicuous position.

3.3 Business Letters

The company name must appear on all business letters, cheques, invoices, statements, receipts and official publications. In addition business letters must show the place of registration, the address of the registered office and the registered number of the company. There is a choice when printing business letters either to print the names of all directors (i.e. either Christian names or initials and surnames) or not to print any of their names. Companies shall not print the names of just some of the directors. Where the business address is not the registered office it is suggested that the former be printed at the top and the latter at the bottom of letterheaded stationery.

If the company is registered for VAT its invoices must show the following: the company name, business address, VAT registration number, number of the invoice, date of supply, description of the supply, amount payable excluding VAT, rate of VAT, amount of VAT, rate of cash discount and the customer's name and address. Much of this information will be either typed or written on the invoice.

3.4 Directors

The section on articles of association (2.4 page 27) dealt with the appointment, powers and remuneration of directors. On incorporation of the company one of the directors may be appointed managing director. No specific powers are accorded to him by law and his authority is based entirely on the terms and conditions imposed on him by the board of directors and his service contract (if any). Regulation 72 of Table A enables the directors to delegate to any managing director such of their powers as they consider desirable to be exercised by him. It is not unusual to entrust him with the day-to-day management of the company, save that he cannot normally exercise the borrowing powers of the company.

Sometimes the articles of association will name the first chairman of the board of directors. If this is not done he can be appointed at the first meeting of the directors to hold office for a certain period or at each individual meeting of the directors to act as chairman of that meeting. The chairman is a director who takes the chair at board and general meetings. He has certain powers normally set out in the articles relating to the conduct of meetings and is given a casting vote in the event of an equality of votes on any matter (Table A regulation 88). Apart from this he has no special powers. Over the years the position of chairman appears to have developed into one of special reverence and tends to be given to the most senior director.

Table A regulation 93 enables a resolution in writing signed by all the directors to be as valid and effective as if it had been passed at a duly convened and held meeting of the directors. This is a very useful provision where it is not always possible to get the directors together for a meeting.

A director of a company cannot also be the company's auditor.

3.5 Secretary

Every company must have a secretary, who may also be a director provided that he is not the sole director. The position of secretary of a private company is an important one and should not be under-estimated. Table A regulation 99 provides for the secretary to be appointed by the directors for such term, at such remuneration and upon such conditions as they may think fit. They may also remove the secretary. As the first secretary must be named in the documents presented to the Registrar of Companies prior to registration his appointment should be minuted at the first meeting of the directors.

As the company's chief administrative officer the secretary has ostensible authority in day-to-day administrative matters. His duties will include the convening of board and company meetings, taking of minutes of meetings, keeping of the company's statutory books so that they are up to date, filing of returns and forms with the Registrar of Companies and dealing with the administrative functions of share transfers, proxies and other forms.

3.6 Accounting Reference Period and Accounts

A company may notify the Registrar of its accounting reference date within six months of the date of its incorporation. This will be the date to which it will make up its accounts each year. If a company fails to make such notification on Form G224 the accounting reference date is 31 March in each year until any subsequent alteration. The first accounting reference period begins on its incorporation and will normally be for a period exceeding six months but not exceeding eighteen months. Accounting reference periods subsequent to the first period begin after the end of the previous accounting reference period and except where it has been altered will be for succeeding periods of twelve months duration.

A company is required by the Companies Act 1985 to keep accounting records to show and explain the company's transactions and disclose with reasonable accuracy the financial position of the company at any particular time. The records must be such as to enable the directors to ensure that any balance sheet and profit and loss account, when set out in the prescribed form for company accounts, give a 'true and fair view' of the state of the company and of its transactions.

The records must be maintained on a day-to-day basis and must (a) show all moneys paid and received by the company and identify the underlying transactions; (b) contain a record of the assets and liabilities of the company; (c) include a statement of the stock of goods held by the company at the end of each financial year and (d) include statements allowing debtors and creditors for goods and services to be identified. These accounting records must be retained by a private company for at least three years.*

* See 3.16, (4) Value Added Tax, page 50 regarding retention of records.

Within ten months of the end of an accounting reference period a private company must lay a full set of accounts before the members in general meeting. These accounts, which must have been audited, will include a balance sheet, profit and loss account and a directors' report. In addition a small company must file a modified balance sheet with the Registrar of Companies. This will not need to incorporate either a directors' report or copy of the profit and loss account. To qualify as 'small' a company must not exceed two of the following three limits — its turnover must not exceed £1,400,000; its gross assets must not exceed £700,000; and its average number of employees for both that year and the previous year must not be more than fifty.

3.7 Auditors

The first auditors of the company may be appointed by the directors before the first general meeting of the company at which accounts are to be laid and they will hold office until the conclusion of that meeting. The qualifications which an auditor must have are that he is either a chartered or certified accountant or a person authorized by the Department of Trade to be appointed as an auditor.

At every annual general meeting a specific resolution appointing or re-appointing the auditors must be passed. It must provide that their term of office should run from the conclusion of the general meeting at which accounts are laid until the conclusion of the next. Where a casual vacancy occurs in the position of auditor the directors may fill this, failing which the company in general meeting may do so. Where a company fails to appoint an auditor, it must give notice to the Secretary of State within 7 days of the general meeting at which the auditor should have been appointed and in those circumstances the Secretary of State may appoint an auditor.

An auditor may be removed from office by ordinary resolution but the auditor may make representations in writing to the company. A dormant company is entitled to dispense with the appointment of auditors.

In a small company the auditor may act as accountant and in this capacity will be involved in preparing the accounts of the company and possibly VAT and PAYE returns and generally in giving taxation and company secretarial assistance. None the less the legal responsibility for this rests with the directors. The auditor's legal duty is to report to the members on whether or not the accounting records of the company have been properly kept and on whether or not the balance sheet and profit and loss account present a true and fair view of the company's affairs and comply with the requirements of the Companies Act 1985

3.8 Statutory Books and Company Seal

In addition to proper books of account it will be necessary after incorporation to maintain a number of statutory registers. A bound or loose leaf combined register can be purchased from most law stationers and will include a register of applications and allotments, a register of transfers, a register of members, a register of directors and secretaries, a register of director's interests, a register of mortgages and charges, a minute book and a book of share certificates. It is the company secretary's responsibility to maintain these registers.

All companies must have a seal engraved with the full name of the company. This seal is the signature of the company and must be impressed upon any documents which would, if executed by a person, be required to be made by deed. These will include contracts for consideration, leases, share certificates, debentures and mortgages. Normally the articles of association will provide that the affixing of the seal be evidenced by the signatures of a director and secretary.

3.9 Issue of Shares

Before issuing shares the directors must ensure that the regulations in the articles of association have been observed (See 2.4, page 26, on articles of association, restrictions on issue of shares and restriction on transfer of shares.) At the board meeting at which shares are issued the secretary will record the issue in the minutes. He will also make the appropriate entries in the register of members to show the names and addresses of all members and particulars of the shares issued. This register is open for inspection to members for two hours daily without charge and to other persons on payment of a small fee.

The entries in the minutes and register apply both to a new issue of shares and to a transfer of shares. The secretary will then complete a share certificate which will be numbered and which will state the number and class of shares which are being issued to each member. This will then be signed by a director and the secretary and the company seal will be impressed on the certificate. The membership of the company is not perfectly constituted until the member's name is duly recorded, in the register of members. The sequence of events is the same for a transfer of shares save that the share transfer form should be checked by the secretary to ensure that the correct stamp duty based on the consideration for the transfer has been paid to the Inland Revenue and the appropriate fee stamp affixed.

3.10 Meetings

Without meetings of directors and members a company could not carry on business. It is thus clear that the regulation of such meetings is a very important part of company law. The method of calling meetings and the proceedings thereat are laid down in the articles of association. It is interesting to compare the number of regulations in Table A relating to members' meetings and directors' meetings respectively. This reveals that directors' meetings are more informal in nature. Regulations 36 to 63 inclusive, a total of twenty eight, govern members' meetings whereas regulations 88 to 98 inclusive, a total of eleven, govern directors' meetings. The informality of directors' meetings is to a great extent caused by the opening sentence of regulations 88 of Table A which reads 'Subject to the provisions of the articles, the directors may regulate their proceedings as they think fit.'

To hold a meeting either of directors or members it is necessary for a minimum number of persons to be present (a quorum). The necessary quorum is usually stated in the articles of association. Regulations 40 and 89 of Table A fix the quorum as two for meetings of members and directors respectively. Where there is to be a sole director it will be necessary to alter or exclude regulation 89 of Table A in the articles.

3.11 Directors' Meetings

No period of notice has been prescribed for the calling of board meetings. Provided that notice is given to all directors a meeting can be summoned in a few minutes or hours.

First Board Meeting
The company exists from the day the Registrar of Companies issues the certificate of incorporation. However until the first board meeting has been held much important business cannot be carried out. Obviously this meeting cannot be held until the date of incorporation but it is wise to hold it on that day or very shortly thereafter. It is suggested that the order of the items on the agenda below is not varied since these are in a logical sequence:

(a) To report the incorporation of the company and produce the certificate of incorporation.
(b) To report the appointment of the first directors and secretary.
(c) To appoint a chairman.

(d) To appoint additional directors (if any).

(e) To report upon the situation of the registered office and if necessary change this.

(f) To adopt a company seal and confirm the authorized users and signatories (the articles usually give authority to a director and secretary).

(g) To open a Bank Account with _____ Bank Plc and to name the signatories, e.g. any two directors or a director and secretary etc. (A company mandate obtainable from any bank will set out the required wording which can be reproduced under this clause.)

In addition to the company mandate the bank will require sight of the certificate of incorporation and will require a copy of the memorandum and articles of association for their retention.

(h) To allot shares (other than subscribers' shares) and to record the receipt of monies for the subscribers' shares and any further shares allotted. To record the sealing of the share certificates issued.

(i) To appoint auditors and decide upon the accounting reference date.

Obviously this meeting can be extended to cover the appointment of solicitors, the disclosure of directors' interest in contracts, the appointment of a managing director and matters connected with the trading activities of the company. The secretary will note the proceedings at this meeting and record them in the minute book. It is suggested that a separate book is kept for the minutes of directors' meetings.

3.12 General Meetings of Members

Members (shareholders) meet together to control the company and to delegate the running of the business to the directors. Their ultimate power to control the company is exercised by resolutions

41

in general meeting. The articles usually provide that voting at meetings is by a show of hands. Each member, regardless of his holding of shares, has one vote on a show of hands. Most articles provide for the chairman, any two members or a member or members holding not less than one-tenth of the total voting rights to demand a poll. When a poll has been demanded voting is normally on the basis of one vote per share held. Where articles provide that different types of shares carry special voting rights these will be taken into account before deciding whether a motion has been carried or not on a poll. A person attending a meeting as a proxy will not normally have a vote on a show of hands but on a poll will have the same voting rights as the person for whom he is proxy. There are two kinds of general meetings:

(1) *Annual General Meeting*
A meeting described as the annual general meeting in the notice convening it must be held in every calendar year, and not more than fifteen months after the holding of the preceding one. A company need not hold its first annual general meeting in the year of its incorporation or the following year provided it is held within eighteen months of incorporation.

The annual general meeting must be called by the secretary giving at least 21 days notice in writing to all members holding shares conferring the right to vote. In counting the days of notice, the day of posting the notice letter and the day of the meeting should be excluded. Proceedings at an annual general meeting called by a shorter notice than the prescribed notice are considered valid provided that all members entitled to attend and vote agree to the short notice.

As previously indicated the proceedings of the meetings of members are more formal than those of board meetings and it is necessary for motions to be proposed, seconded and then voted upon. The main matters dealt with at the annual general meeting are as follows:

(a) To receive the accounts and the directors' report.
(b) To propose a dividend.

(c) To re-elect directors who retire by rotation.
(d) To re-elect the auditors and fix their remuneration.

(2) *Extraordinary General Meetings*

General meetings other than the annual general meeting are known as extraordinary general meetings. They are usually convened by the secretary, on the instructions of the directors, where any business is to be transacted that cannot wait until the next annual general meeting. These meetings require at least 14 days' notice except where a special resolution is to be considered when the notice required is 21 days. Short notice of the meeting can be accepted where a majority in number of members agree provided they in aggregate hold at least 95 per cent in nominal value of the voting shares.

Every company must keep minutes of all proceedings of general meetings in books kept for that purpose and such minutes when signed by the chairman of the meeting or of the next succeeding meeting are evidence of the proceedings. These minutes are normally held in a minute book which must be kept at the registered office and be open to free inspection by any member during business hours for at least two hours in each day.

3.13 Mortgages, Charges and Debentures

Since these all involve the borrowing of money it is necessary for the secretary to check that the directors are not exceeding the amount they can borrow* without the prior consent of the shareholders before the transaction is finalized by signing and sealing the appropriate document.

Every charge (which includes a mortgage) created by a company has to be registered at the Companies Registry within 21 days of its creation. Included in this requirement are a charge for the

* See 2.4, page 28 re powers of directors.

purpose of securing any issue of debentures, a floating charge on the undertaking or property of the company and a charge on land or any interest in land. Unless registered such charges will be void against the liquidator and any creditor of the company so far as any security on the company's properly or undertaking is conferred thereby, and the moneys secured immediately become repayable. The company and every officer of the company who is in default in registering the instruments will also be liable to a fine of £100 a day during the continuance of the default. Holders of unregistered debentures are reduced to the position of unsecured creditors of the company.

A copy of the certificate of registration, issued by the Registrar of Companies, must be endorsed on every debenture or certificate of debenture stock issued by the company unless the charge was created after the issue. When a registered charge has been repaid or satisfied a 'memorandum of satisfaction' should be filed with the registrar. This is in the interest of the company and accordingly the company secretary should always be instructed to deal with this.

In addition to the record of mortgages and charges maintained at the Companies Registry every company must keep a register of all charges specifically affecting its property, and all floating charges on the undertaking or any property of the company. Any creditor or member of the company has a right to inspect the copies of the instruments creating registrable charges and the register of charges kept by the company. Any other person may only inspect the register of charges on payment of a small fee. The company must enter in the register a short description of the property charged, the amount of the charge, and the names of the persons entitled thereto, except in the case of securities to bearer.

When a company acquires property charged as above it must be registered within 21 days of completion of the acquisition. When a Scottish company mortgages English property, particulars must be filed in England as well as Scotland. A corresponding obligation is imposed upon English companies mortgaging Scottish property.

3.14 Annual Returns

Every company must each year file a return, called an 'annual return', with the Registrar of Companies (Form A363). This return must be made up to the fourteenth day after the annual general meeting for the year. It will include the address of the registered office, full details of the nominal and issued shares, the amount of the indebtedness of the company in respect of all mortgages and charges, a full list of present members and of all persons who have ceased to be members since the date of the last return, including the number of shares held and transferred since the date of the last annual return, and full details of the directors and secretary. A copy of the annual return signed by a director and the secretary must be sent to the registrar, with the registration fee of £20, within 42 days of the annual general meeting. If an annual general meeting is not held in a particular year (apart from the year of incorporation), a return must still be filed, made up to the 31 December.

3.15 Register of Directors' Interests in Shares or Debentures of the Company

In addition to the register of directors and secretaries which every limited company must keep at its registered office containing full details of all directors and secretaries, a register must also be kept into which full details of directors' interests in shares or debentures must be entered.

A director of a company must notify the company of any interest he has in its shares or debentures, the acquisition or cessation of any such interest, and the grant, exercise or assignment of any right to subscribe for shares or debentures of any holding company or subsidiary of the company. The company must be notified within 14 days of any dealings which give rise to or terminate such interests or rights of subscription. Newly appointed directors possessing such interests or rights must notify the company of them within 14 days of their appointment. The above mentioned

45

requirement extends to and includes interests of wives, husbands or infant children of a director, and dealings in those interests, and notification must be made accordingly. All the information and details referred to above must be entered in the register which must be open for inspection by members of the company without charge and by other persons upon payment of a small inspection charge. In addition the register must be produced at the beginning of, and remain accessible to any person attending, the company's annual general meeting.

3.16 Taxation

Although it is beyond the scope of this book to deal with the complex and changeable subject of taxation it is desirable for the owners of a private company to have a basic knowledge of the various types of tax payable and to be aware of simple ways to mitigate and delay the date of the tax liability.

(1) *Corporation Tax*
Unlike the sole trader or partner in a partnership who is chargeable to income tax based on the profits of the business in the previous year (other than in the opening or closing years of a business) a private company pays corporation tax. Each year in the budget the Chancellor of the Exchequer will normally announce the rates of corporation tax for the financial year ended that 31 March. In the March 1984 budget, however, the rates of corporation tax for the years ending 31 March 1984, 1985, 1986 and 1987 were announced.

Assessments to corporation tax are made on a company by reference to accounting periods. Thus if a company makes its accounts up to the 30 September each year half of its profits may be payable at one rate and the other half at another rate if the rate of corporation tax has been changed for either financial year.

For example, if a company made its accounts up to the 30 September 1983 and its profits assessable to corporation tax was less than £100,000, then half of its assessment would be at the rate of 38 per cent (financial year ended 31 March 1983) and half at the rate of 30 per cent (financial year ended 31 March 1984).

There are two rates of corporation tax, the small companies rate for companies with profits of £100,000 or less and the normal rate. For the financial year ended 31 March 1985 these are 30 per cent and 45 per cent respectively. The general rule is that corporation tax for an accounting period must be paid within nine months of the end of that period.

When a private company is registered the Inspector of Taxes will normally send to the registered office of the company a Form CT41G, requesting certain information. If this is not received the directors should request the form from the tax office most local to the registered office of the company. The form requires the following information:

(a) The nature of the activities of the company.
(b) (i) The address of its registered office.
    (ii) The place of business if different to the address in b(i).
(c) The date of commencement of business.
(d) If an existing business has taken over, the name and address of that business and the name and address of the person from whom the business was acquired.
(e) The date to which the first accounts will be prepared.
(f) The name and address of the accountants dealing with the company's affairs.
(g) If PAYE is already operated the name of the tax district and full reference number.

The inspector will also require a copy of the memorandum and articles of association.

It is important that thought is give to the answer to question (e) as the date when payment of tax is due can be delayed by the careful selection of this date. This particularly applies where the business is seasonal. This can best be explained by an example.

Example
A.J. Fireworks Ltd is incorporated and commences business on

1 November 1983 manufacturing fireworks which it sells to retailers. In the year to 31 October 1984 it makes profits of £80,000. If the company chooses 31 October as its accounting reference date the tax on £80,000 namely £24,000 would be payable on 31 July 1985. However since virtually all this profit was earned in September and October 1984 it is interesting to note the effect of making accounts up to 31 August 1984.

Accounting reference date 31 August

Profits to 31 August 1984	£5,000
Profits to 31 August 1985	£75,000
Tax payable 31 May 1985	£1,500
Tax payable 31 May 1986	£22,500

In this example although the total tax liability is the same the company has enjoyed the use of £22,500 for ten months. Although it may be felt that this is an extreme example there are many seasonal businesses which earn much of their profits in the months preceding Christmas and others in the summer rather than the winter months.

Another consideration regarding the date when the tax is payable is cash flow. If tax is payable when stocks are low rather than high the money should be more readily available to meet the tax liability. Whereas if the tax is payable when the company's liquid funds are invested in high stocks a cash flow problem may be encountered.

Another means of delaying the payment of tax is the first year allowances on plant and machinery (other than motor cars). These are however being phased out and will cease to apply to expenditure on plant and machinery after 31 March 1986. If a business which earned profits of £20,000 needed to invest in new machinery to the value of £20,000, it would reduce its taxable profits to nil by purchasing this machinery just before the end of the current accounting year rather than purchasing it in the first month of the following year.

It should be noted that if a private company is being formed to take over the business owned and operated by the promoters of the company, thought needs to be given to the date of the change. This is due to the closing provisions for income tax which apply when a business ceases trading for tax purposes. Careful planning of the date can achieve an income tax saving or ensure that no unnecessary additional liability is incurred.

(2) *The Imputation System*

Where a company makes a distribution of profits by way of a dividend to shareholders, the company is liable to pay an amount of corporation tax, known as 'advance corporation tax'. The rate of advance corporation tax is determined annually in the Finance Act. A company is required to make quarterly returns and an additional return at the accounting date where that date does not coincide with a quarterly date. Payment of the advance corporation tax is due when lodging the return. This tax is then deductible by the company from any corporation tax payable in respect of any income for that accounting period. Where the company does not make any distributions by way of dividend no return need be made for that period.

(3) *Pay As You Earn (PAYE)*

This operates in the same way for a private company as for a sole trader or partnership which employs staff. The only difference is that the owner/director of a private company is regarded as an employee for PAYE* and National Insurance (NI)** purposes and accordingly these must be deducted from any remuneration drawn. This contrasts with the position of the sole trader who pays Schedule D income tax twice a year on 1 January and 1 July including national insurance class 4 contributions. In addition the

* Further details of PAYE requirements will be found in *Employers Guide to PAYE* issued by the Board of Inland Revenue (P8).
** Further details of national insurance contributions requirements will be found in the *Employers Guide NP15* issued by the Department of Health and Social Security.

49

sole trader pays the self-employed fixed rate national insurance stamp. It should be noted that the aggregate of the national insurance contributions of the private company and director payable on his remuneration are larger than those payable by the sole trader on the equivalent profits.

PAYE and national insurance can be delayed by the owner/director drawing a low salary on a monthly basis and being voted a larger bonus when the companies accounts are prepared. This will also result in the retention of liquid funds in the company.

(4) *Value Added Tax (VAT)*

Where an existing business, which is registered for VAT, is transferred to a private company the latter will have to register for VAT* if the annual registration limit of £19,500 or quarterly limit of £6,500 are exceeded. If a company's turnover is below the registration limits registration is optional. This option is beneficial to a small exporting company which manufactures or purchases its merchandise in the United Kingdom on which it pays VAT but exports to countries, other than the Isle of Man, where the export is zero-rated. In these circumstances if the company registers for VAT it can apply for a monthly, rather than the normal three-monthly period which will enable the company to recover the VAT incurred more quickly, thus creating a cash flow advantage.

From July 1985 VAT records and accounts must be kept of all transactions for six years.

Before a private company, registered for VAT, prints invoices it is desirable to study appendix F to Notice 700 available from HM Customs and Excise or to contact a local customs and excise officer for advice on the requirements.** This will avoid the expense of reprinting the invoices should required items be omitted.

---

* Further details of VAT requirements will be found in *Notice No 700 VAT General Guide* available from HM Customs and Excise.

** See 3.3 Business Letters

3.17 Changes after Incorporation

Various changes may take place after incorporation which will involve the filing of various forms or copies of resolutions. Amongst these are the following:

Change of Directors or Secretary
Whenever a change occurs in the directors or secretary or in their particulars it is necessary to file a Form G288 (Notice of change of directors or secretaries or in their particulars). In addition to the full details the form must contain a signed consent by any persons named as a new director(s) or secretary that they agree to act in their respective capacities. The completed form signed by a director or secretary must be filed with the Registrar of Companies within 14 days of the change.

Change of Registered Office
Any change must be notified within 14 days on a Form G287 which has to state the full address and must be signed by a director or secretary.

Increase in Capital and Allotment of Shares
Where the capital of a company is increased a copy of the ordinary resolution authorizing the increase together with a Form G123 giving particulars of the increase must be filed within 15 days of the resolution being passed. No duty is payable.

Within one month of the allotment of shares a return of allotments form must be completed and filed with the Registrar of Companies. Where the consideration for the issue is cash the form to be completed is PUC2. In the case of non-cash consideration the required form is PUC3 which must be accompanied either by a written contract or by the prescribed particulars on Form G88(3). Duty at the rate of £1 per £100 or part of £100 is payable on registration of these forms. However no capital duty is payable if a company makes a bonus issue of shares out of undistributed profits.

Change of Company Name

A copy of the special resolution of the company authorizing the change of name together with the registration fee of £40 must be filed with the Registrar of Companies. The name of the company does not change until the date on which the Registrar of Companies issues the certificate on change of name.

Changes in the Contents of the Memorandum and Articles of Association

A copy of the special resolution authorizing the change together with a copy of the memorandum or articles of association as altered must be filed within 15 days with the Registrar of Companies.

3.18 Reregistration of an Unlimited Company as Limited

Where a company has been registered as an unlimited company (see 1.1, page 4) it is possible to reregister it as a limited company. This cannot however be done if the company has previously been converted from limited to unlimited.

Before such a change it is necessary to pass a special resolution of the company stating that it shall be reregistered as limited. The resolution should also state particulars as to the share capital and detail the amendments to the memorandum and articles of association. In addition an application to the Registrar of Companies must be made on Form G51. The registration fee payable is the same as for the incorporation of a new company. Capital duty is payable on the net value of the assets of any kind belonging to the company immediately after reregistration or the nominal value of the issued shares, whichever is the higher. On receipt of the documents the Registrar of Companies will issue a revised certificate of incorporation.

3.19 Reregistration of a Limited Company as Unlimited

This can be done only after all the members of the limited company have indicated their approval for the reregistration on Form G49(8)(a). In addition the memorandum and articles of association must be altered to bring them into conformity with Table E of the Companies (Tables A to F) Regulations 1985. The forms to be filed are: (a) Form G49(1), being the application to reregister as an unlimited company, which must be signed by a director or secretary; (b) Form G49(8)(a), signed by all members of the limited company; (c) Form G49(8)(b), a statutory declaration signed by all the directors indicating that Form G49(8)(a) has been signed by all the members, and (d) a printed copy of the memorandum and articles of association as altered.

On receipt of these documents and the £5 re-registration fee the Registrar of Companies will issue a revised certificate of incorporation.

3.20 Winding Up of a Private Company

Dissolution
A company can be 'dissolved' by resolution of the members or creditors or by a petition through the court. The final act of dissolution is preceded by a process called winding up or liquidation.

There are three types of liquidation:
(i)   members' voluntary;
(ii) creditors' voluntary and
(iii) compulsory winding up by the court.
In (i) and (ii) the winding up is called 'voluntary' because the members in (i) and the creditors in (ii) take the initiative to wind up the company without the intervention of the court. If a petition is presented in the court for a company to be wound up and the court makes an order, the winding up is called 'compulsory'. However whichever form the liquidation takes during the course of the liquidation the

directors' powers cease and the company is managed by a liquidator who is a person appointed by whichever group initiates the winding up.

The task of the liquidator is to realize what he can from the company's assets and draw up accounts showing what is available to pay creditors and how much and when they are paid. Any funds remaining after the creditors and liquidator have been paid are divided among the shareholders.

Being Struck Off

A company can be dissolved by being struck off the official register of companies by the Registrar of Companies under sections 652 and 653 of the Companies Act 1985. This process usually commences because a company has not filed annual returns. In the first instance, the registrar sends the company a letter stating that he has reasonable grounds to believe that the company is not carrying on business or operating and inquiring whether or not this is the case. If no answer is received to that letter the registrar sends further letters and finally strikes the company name off the index. In these circumstances ownership of the assets of the company, if any, will pass to the Crown, Duchy of Lancaster or the Duke of Cornwall as the case may be. The directors' or members' right to deal with the assets of the company is forfeited and can be regained only by having the company name restored to the index through the courts.

Where a company is no longer trading and has no assets or liabilities the directors may request the Registrar of Companies to strike the company name off the index to avoid the cost of a voluntary liquidation.

Part IV
Starting the Business of the Company

Your company has now been formed and you are ready to draw up your plans to commence trading. Having decided that you can make the business work, you will need to have researched all the elements that go into running a successful business:

(a) What goods or products you are planning to manufacture or market.

(b) What services you will be offering.

(c) What the direct costs of purchasing or manufacturing the goods or products are, including raw materials.

(d) How much they will cost to produce after allowing for all general overheads (rent, rates, water, light, heat, telephone, postages, staff salaries and national insurance, advertising, travelling expenses, insurance, legal, accountancy and audit costs).

(e) At what price the products or services will sell in order to generate sufficient custom and volume of sales to make the business profitable.

(f) How much capital will be needed to finance the business.

(g) Where and how finance can be raised.

(h) What type of premises are required and where these should be located.

(i) What insurance is required by law.

(j) What insurance should be taken out voluntarily.

(k) What the best methods are of marketing the products and/or services.

(l) What the regulations are concerning the employment of staff.

(m) Is the company required to register for VAT?

(n) Does the company need an export licence and if so how this is obtained?

All these and many more questions will need to be answered and it is unlikely that any one person or source of information will be able to provide all the necessary answers.

So where do we start?

4.1 Advisers

Very few people starting in business, however competent they may be, will be able to get a new enterprise off the ground without proper advice. In recent years successive governments have been committed to the encouragement of enterprise and in particular to the giving of free assistance and advice to small firms. They have realized that small firms have the potential to offer employment, innovation, diversity and future growth and see this sector as the seed corn of future economic prosperity. For this reason emphasis has been placed by government, local council and a variety of private sector organizations on advisory services and counselling so that the small business man may have access to the most expert and timely advice possible.

4.2 Small Firms Service

This service is run by the Department of Trade and Industry and was set up by the government to encourage and assist new small firms and businesses. It is designed to improve the availability of information and advice. The service is also available to medium-sized existing firms.

The service is operated from twelve small firms centres in England, Wales and Scotland.* A telephone call to your local centre will be dealt with by an enquiry officer who will discuss your needs and initially will send out a 'Start up information package' consisting of booklets covering *Starting Your Own Business — The*

* See Appendix III.

56

Practical Steps, Running Your Own Business — Planning for Success, Elements of Book-keeping, Small Business Loan Guarantee Scheme, details of the business counselling information and management advice and a copy of the most recent *In Business Now*, a periodical newspaper giving news for small and growing businesses. If your requirements are for more detailed information serveral other booklets are available on *Employing People, Management Accounting, Marketing, How to Start Exporting, Selling to Large Firms, Microprocessors and the Small Business* and *Insurance.*

The advice available is supplied in two ways:

(a) Once a month the centres hold small business advice days between 10 a.m. and 4 p.m. at various job centres where an enquiry officer and a business counsellor are available to supply information and answer a wide range of business questions.

(b) Where your enquiry is detailed you may be invited to meet a small firms business counsellor. The counsellors are people with considerable business experience, chosen by the Department of Trade and Industry to provide advisory services to small firms. Many have held senior positions in general management and have been successful in small- or medium-sized businesses. The first three sessions for counselling are free and each session will be for a duration of one to one-and-half hours. If further sessions are required, a modest charge is made.

This service provides information relating to any business problem ranging from finance, diversification and industrial training to exporting, planning, technological advances, industrial relations, marketing and, broadly speaking, any kind of business administration enquiry. The counsellor may be able to assist with the preparation of a 'business plan' and 'cash flow forecast' both of which are important when a bank or other financial institution is approached for loan finance.

In Scotland and Wales the small firms service is operated

through the Scottish Development Agency and Welsh Development Agency in co-operation with the Scottish and Welsh Offices.

Although the small firms service will discuss your problems with you and offer advice and guidance, the course of action you ultimately take must be based on your own commercial judgement after consulting your own professional advisers. It is a condition of accepting the service that neither the business counsellor nor the government department or agency providing the service can be held liable for any loss or liability which may be incurred as a result of any advice or inaccurate information given negligently or otherwise by a business counsellor or a member of the staff of a small firms centre.

4.3 Local Enterprise Agencies

'Business in the Community' can supply the name, address and telephone number of any of the 196 Enterprise Agencies operating locally throughout England, Wales, Scotland and Northern Ireland. These are non-profit making organizations backed by the district and county councils, local and national businesses, the banks and chambers of commerce. They aim to encourage and help people to start and run successful businesses by offering a free counselling service. They are also sometimes able to provide initial free professional advice, guidance and expertise from the considerable resources of their supporting organizations.

This service may include assistance with starting or expanding a business, problems of an existing business, marketing, finance, premises, personnel and employment legislation, accountancy, tax and VAT, business plans, training, insurance, legal matters and planning permission. In view of the counsellor's local knowledge he can provide invaluable help with local marketing, suitable premises and names of local banks which are more likely to be able to offer finance whether long or short term. He will also be able to assist with the preparation of a 'business plan' and 'cash flow forecast' that will be required by the bank manager before entertaining a start up loan. It is interesting to note that 6–10 per cent of enquiries to the enterprise agencies originate from customers passed to them by the banks.

A recent survey by 'Business in the Community', the 'umbrella' organization of the Enterprise Agencies show that they are currently helping to create jobs at the rate of 30,000 a year and that they assist in 76 start-ups a year and conduct 530 counselling sessions devoting 70 per cent of time to new business and 30 per cent to existing business. With the additional agencies planned it is anticipated that these figures will grow rapidly.

In addition to the counselling service the local enterprise agencies organize and hold courses, seminars and exhibitions on a variety of subjects connected with starting and running a business. Publicity to those offering help to small businesses is given during local enterprise week held annually in May or June. This week attracts considerable local press, television and radio coverage of the events and shows the small business community the wide range of help now on offer locally.

4.4 Council for Small Industries in Rural Areas (CoSIRA)

CoSIRA is the main agent of the Development Commission whose prime objective is to help the rural parts of England support viable and prospective communities and thus improve the general quality of life, especially in areas where the population is declining or which are in other ways disadvantaged. In support of this aim CoSIRA is charged with improving the prosperity of small businesses in the countryside by providing a local source of advice backed up by technical and management services, training facilities and assistance in obtaining funds from the banks, Investment in Industry Plc and from its own resources. CoSIRA has representatives (known as small industries organizers) who are stationed in every English county. Together with a voluntary committee they can provide assistance with a wide variety of problems affecting the small firm.

Normally small manufacturing and servicing businesses and in certain areas, small tourism enterprises providing overnight accommodation (small hotels, guest houses, motels and holiday chalets) are eligible for assistance from CoSIRA.

4.5 Specialist Business and Technical Advice

The Department of Trade and Industry provides specialist technical advice through such services as the small firms technical enquiry service, the quality assurance advisory service, the design council's design advisory service funded consultancy scheme and the energy advisory services. These services provide free advice or consultancy:

(a) For small manufacturing businesses which have come across a technical or production problem.
(b) To help companies to obtain quality assurance approval from a recognized authority.
(c) To any manufacturer on all aspects of product design.
(d) On the basic measures necessary for the implementation and development of any energy management programme which will enable firms to reduce their energy costs and lead to increased profits.

These services are available from the Department of Trade and Industry regional offices.

4.6 Libraries

A visit to a main library can be a surprisingly beneficial journey. Most main libraries incorporate a reference library where the librarian will be able to supply you with a list of books on starting a business and the various aspects thereof which may be of interest.

Much of the reference information will be on microfiche which enables the librarian to give you a more efficient and quicker service. You can then either study the appropriate books there or borrow them from the lending library. Many reference libraries have Prestel (a visual information service operated by British Telecom) which provides quick access to a large range of business and start up information.

Most trades and businesses have one or more periodical journals which if not available at the reference library can be obtained from a local newsagent, after you have ascertained at the library the name of the publication and of the publisher. The library may also have information on local county industry and business publications which make interesting reading. These publications, in conjunction with the local council, organize regular exhibitions. A visit to one of these exhibitions will be an opportunity to examine the latest technology, new ideas and products and to establish new business contacts. These exhibitions invariably incorporate seminars on a variety of business subjects and show Video Arts training films (starring John Cleese) on improving management and sales techniques.

Additionally you will be able to find information of the services provided by the local Chamber of Commerce. Like libraries the Chambers of Commerce have improved with time and many now offer advice, training, seminars, trade directories, periodical business newsletters and other services to members.

4.7 The Bank Manager

A good bank manager can give advice on many business and commercial matters, not necessarily on those limited to finance. He will have a good knowledge of local affairs and businesses and probably has the backing of a central information and advice service. The manager should be kept informed of the plans for the business and of its progress. However, when the manager is being approached to provide start up or ongoing finance for the business it is advisable to use the advisory services of the small firms service, a local enterprise agency or an accountant to assist in preparing a business plan and cash flow forecast. The applicant for finance who draws up a careful plan will stand a better chance of success than someone who breezes in with grandiose plans but no hard facts.

Although there is no hard-and-fast rule thereon, banks may make a charge for management time spent on advising customers in relation to business matters. This may be included in the amount for bank charges debited to the customer's account.

4.8 The Accountant

One of the main reasons for the failure of businesses in their early years is that the owners fail to keep proper records to give them valuable up-to-date information concerning the activities and results of the business. Many businessmen still regard their accountant as a necessary evil who prepares historical accounts well after the year end for statutory purposes. These persons ignore the important part that a good accountant can play in setting up the necessary records required to prepare regular management accounts. The availability of these will enable the owners to take important decisions based on knowledge rather than guesswork.

Management accounts, although similar in layout to the annual audited accounts, will be prepared weekly, monthly or three monthly depending upon the nature and needs of the business. They need to be prepared within six days of the end of the period to be reported upon, if the information they produce is to be acted on. Because of the little time available for their preparation they will be less accurate than annual accounts and many items of expenditure will need to be based on precalculated estimates. Items such as rent, rates, insurance and professional charges can be estimated as can light and heat by reading the meters.

Where the accountant has set up the mechanics to produce

regular management accounts he should be approached before the accounting year end with the figures, since he may be able to suggest ways to mitigate taxation which would be lost if left to the date when the annual accounts are available.

The services of an accountant do not come cheaply but the cost will be justified if the advice received results in improved profitability of the business and mitigation of the tax payable thereon.

The accountant like the bank manager has experience of many different businesses and trades and accordingly his advice need not be sought solely on book-keeping, accounting and taxation matters. He may be able to advise on raising capital, computerization of records, buying and selling a business, national insurance and statutory sickness pay, stock and cash control and many other commercial matters.

4.9 The Solicitor

Like that of accountants, the services of a solicitor can be expensive, but the advantages of proper legal advice should justify the cost. The vast volume of legislation affecting industry and commerce is too complex for the busy layman to have the time to gain the expertise to understand it all. Even solicitors will tend to specialize in one of the many branches of the law. It is therefore important to employ the services of a solicitor knowledgeable in commercial and employment law. The records section of the Law Society will be able to suggest the names of local firms of solicitors who specialize in any branch of the law.

Solicitors in addition to dealing with the conveyance of premises and leases will be able to advise on contract law, the law regarding the sale of goods, the Trades Description Act 1968, the Fair Trading Act 1973 under which the Director-General of Fair Trading may investigate trading practices which may lead to customers being misled, advertising standards, the law with regard to employing and dismissing staff, the law regarding health and safety of employees and other people whilst on the firm's premises or work site, air pollution, creating unnecessary noise, discharge of noxious materials, the hours during which shops may open, the Landlord and Tenant Act 1954, planning permission, change of use of business premises and the collection of money from slow-paying debtors.

4.10 ACAS: The Advisory, Conciliation and Arbitration Service

This is an independent body charged with the duty of promoting the improvement of industrial relations. It seeks to discharge this responsibility through the voluntary co-operation of employers, employees and their representatives but it has no powers of compulsion. The service is free and is supplied by people with special experience of industrial relations. Employers, employees and trade unions can approach ACAS separately or jointly on all matters connected with employment. ACAS also publishes various booklets which are available from any ACAS office.

4.11 Finance

When considering the finance required to start trading it will be necessary to take into account the cost of premises, fixtures, fittings, plant and equipment and other permanent assets needed to establish the business. To this will be added the cost of professional advice and expenses and promotional expenses including advertising. Thirdly must be added the cost of stock and/or raw materials. Finally must be taken into account working capital to cover trading costs for a period of, say, three to six months to include salaries for the proprietors to cover their living expenses and a contingency allowance. The sum of these will represent the total capital required.

The next stage before considering what type of finance is

required (long, medium or short term) and the source of the funds, is to prepare your case for the bank manager or other financial institution. The presentation should be as clear and concise as possible. It should include: full details of the business and how it will operate; details of the experience and qualifications of the proprietors and any key employees; details of the market place for the company's products; details of the main competitors if appropriate to the type of business; the business plan; the cash flow projection and details of the amount of money required; the repayment plan which will be based on the anticipated profit and cash flow forecast and, finally, details of the proprietors' capital and of any security that they are able to offer.

It is worth mentioning that if you are requiring working capital or finance for short-lived assets you probably require short-term finance (up to two years). If you require finance to purchase assets with a medium life you will require medium-term finance (two to seven years) and if the requirement is to purchase buildings, leases and land you will require long-term finance (eight years and over).

4.12 The Banks

Most banks have schemes for helping the new business and also the expanding business. These schemes are geared to provide funds from one to twenty years. Term loans as these are often called, vary both with regard to the upper limit and maximum length of the repayment period. Interest may be at a fixed or variable rate with the monthly repayments constant, movements in the rates being accommodated in the length of the repayment period.

In order to get the best deal possible it is wise to shop around the different banks and compare the amounts they are prepared to lend, the interest rates charged, provisions for repayment and the security they require. These schemes should not be confused with the normal overdraft facility which remains the most versatile form of finance available, since within limits the amount borrowed can fluctuate from day to day. Interest on overdrafts is charged on each day's outstanding balance and is normally cheaper than any other form of external finance.

An example of business start-up loans is that available from Barclays Bank Plc. This is aimed at helping the entrepreneur with a new product or idea but not enough capital to finance start-up costs. It differs from other loans because interest is linked to sales and it is therefore possible to pay relatively little in the first year or two of the business. It can cover capital assets, research and development costs and the loan can be for any amount up to £100,000. Interest is payable in the form of a royalty linked to sales with the capital repayable at the end of the term, normally five years. At the end of the term the capital can be repaid or may be replaced with a more convenient loan. The bank will require some form of assurance concerning the repayment of the loan and will want to see that the borrower is personally making a serious financial commitment to the new enterprise. Normally only business assets will be charged to the bank as security.

4.13 Loan Guarantee Scheme (LGS)

This was introduced in June 1981 as a three-year experiment to assist those new or existing businesses which found it difficult to raise finance under conventional terms. This scheme has now been extended until 31 December 1985. The main terms of the scheme remain unchanged with the Department of Trade and Industry, on behalf of the Secretary of State, being prepared to guarantee repayment of 70 per cent of loans made by participating lenders (the banks and various financial institutions). The LGS is designed to help potentially viable small businesses, particularly those unable to provide security or with no track record, to raise medium-term loans from banks and other financial institutions where these are not available on normal commercial terms. It is not intended as a substitute for conventional forms of lending. Applicants are therefore expected to have considered and actively sought alternative finance before submitting an LGS application. Those unwilling to use personal assets as security for normal forms of lending will not usually be able to raise loans under the LGS. Personal assets will not be taken as security for a scheme loan. The successful borrower will have to supply the lender with further information to enable him to monitor the performance of the business on a regular basis. A premium of 5 per cent per annum on the amount guaranteed is charged which is equivalent to a 3.5 per cent per annum premium on the reducing balance of the loan.

Loans under the scheme may be for amounts of up to £75,000 repayable over periods between two and seven years. Any of the banks or financial institutions participating in the LGS will give advice on the scheme.

4.14 The Smaller Business Loan Scheme in Conjunction with CoSIRA*

Any companies located in the English countryside or in country towns, with a population of up to 10,000, are eligible to apply for a loan under the scheme. They must not employ more than 20 skilled persons although the number of unskilled employees is unlimited. Full details of eligible trades is available from CoSIRA.

Basically, the scheme provides financial assistance in the form of a loan for new or established businesses. The amount available is between £2,000 and £250,000 with between two and twenty years in which to repay the loan. Interest can be fixed or variable. In certain circumstances repayment of the capital may be deferred for up to two years. Security is subject to discussion and loans under ten years may be unsecured.

The scheme is operated by Barclays Bank Plc and National Westminster Bank Plc in conjunction with CoSIRA to whom application for details can be made.

* See page 59 for information on CoSIRA.

4.15 Business Expansion Scheme (BES)

Another government innovation in the field of finance for new companies is the Business Expansion Scheme. The scheme enables an investor to obtain relief against his highest rate of income tax on up to £40,000 invested in any one year, provided the investment is held for five years in an approved business. The scheme includes almost all manufacturing, construction and service industries, including the retail and wholesale trades, the main exclusions being companies involved in financial services, overseas companies and, since March 1985, development companies which have an interest in the land or property that is being developed. For 1985/86 the scheme has been extended to allow companies carrying on research and development to qualify by removing the restrictions on the receipt of royalties for such activities.

The scheme is intended for outside investors rather than for the operator putting funds into his own company; but an investor can qualify if he and his associates own less than 30 per cent of the share capital of a company. A short list of some of the companies specializing in providing this form of venture capital is given in Appendix III.

4.16 Investors in Industry Plc (3i)

Investors in Industry Plc, previously known as Industrial and Commercial Finance Corporation (ICFC), is owned by the major English and Scottish clearing banks and the Bank of England. 3i is an independent private sector company which raises international and domestic money by bond issues and through its network of offices covering the whole country lends to small and medium-sized companies. It provides permanent and long-term investment capital in a variety of forms and will organize a package to meet the individual requirements of the applicant.

3i can provide loans, subscribe for ordinary or preference shares or combine the two. Loan periods may vary between five and twenty years and interest rates can be fixed, variable or a mixture of both. Loan agreements will also cover repayment terms, i.e. by instalments or at the end of the loan period, and can include 'capital holidays' – periods of interest-only repayments in the early years. Any investment in the capital of a new company will be a minority share in the equity and will not be subject to a personal guarantee.

3i is agent for the European Investment Bank (EIB) which provides special low-interest loans for amounts up to £4.25 million on up to 50 per cent of capital expenditure by companies in the assisted areas engaged in manufacturing or selected service activities which will create or safeguard jobs. In addition 3i can make loans from funds provided by the European Coal and Steel Community (ECSC). To be eligible a project need not be directly connected with the coal or steel industries but it must be located in an area where redundancy has occurred in these industries since Britain joined the EEC. The project should create jobs suitable for redundant coalminers or steelworkers. Interest rates are below market rates and an ECSC loan can fund up to 50 per cent of the fixed asset element of a project. Similar loans are also available from the European Coal and Steel Community towards the capital expenditure involved in converting commercial boilers to coal-burning.

4.17 Local Authorities

A wide variety of assistance is available to companies from local authorities. These vary from area to area and it is therefore necessary to enquire from the appropriate local authority about the assistance available. Some have funds from which they can make loans of up to 90 per cent of the cost of land, building and site works on commercial terms for up to thirty years. Some can give grants and loans to help with rents and site preparation. Many local authorities have taken the initiative to try to stimulate industrial development in their areas and to create new jobs particularly in new companies and start-up situations.

In addition many of the new towns have development corporations which take a particular interest in encouraging the development of small firms by building small premises, supplying communal commercial services and providing business advisory services.

4.18 Other Government Support for Business

The Department of Trade and Industry offers industry and commerce direct support through a variety of measures which have now been brought together under four headings

(a) Support for Business and Technical Advisory Services.
(b) Support for Innovation.
(c) Support for National and Regional Investment.
(d) Support for Exports.

There are many measures of support under each heading which are now presented together to help firms identify those which may best suit their needs. In all there are sixty-four schemes for assisting small companies. Many of the schemes are available to companies starting up in the 'assisted areas' and they provide low-cost loans, grants and free advice.

The range of financial assistance available from government sources is too large to detail in this book and so a telephone call to the new central enquiry point which is manned by experts is recommended. See Appendix III under 'Department of Trade and Industry – Support for Business Information Service'.

4.19 Leasing

Leasing takes several forms including finance leasing, operating leasing and contract hire. Under all these the leasing company (the lessor) retains ownership of the asset concerned for the term of the lease. The company entering into the leasing contract (the lessee) has possession and use of the asset in return for the payment of a rental charge over a period of time. As the owner of the asset the lessor obtains the benefit of capital allowances on the cost of the asset which he can pass on to the lessee with lower rental charges.

In 1984 member companies of the Equipment Leasing Association (ELA), the principal trade association for the sector, leased over £4 billion worth of new plant and equipment. One of the reasons for the popularity of leasing is that it usually provides finance for the whole cost of an asset unlike other systems of payment by instalment where the amount provided towards the cost of the asset only matches that provided by the company itself. Another reason is that this method of financing the acquisition of plant, equipment and motor vehicles is of value to the new growing company as it enables the company to plan cash flow with a greater degree of certainty and to conserve working capital for other demands on its funds.

By leasing, a company enjoys the use of the asset and obtains tax relief on the rental charge but does not increase its borrowing. There is also a high degree of flexibility in negotiating the terms of a lease and this enables a company which is subject to seasonal variations in its cash flow to reflect these variations when agreeing the timing of the rental charges.

As with all forms of finance, costs vary considerably and accordingly it is prudent to obtain several comparable quotes before making a decision to enter into any leasing contract.

4.20 Hire Purchase

Most private individuals are familiar with hire purchase. Documentation is usually standard so that the finance can be obtained fairly quickly subject to a check on the creditworthiness of the borrower.

The hire purchase company technically purchases the particular asset involved and then hires it to the company, which makes an initial down-payment of 20–25 per cent of the cost and regular payments of a fixed amount over an agreed term. The asset remains the property of the hire purchase company until the client company pays a nominal purchase price at the end of the agreement period. From a taxation point of view, hire purchase differs from leasing as the company can obtain capital allowances on the asset and relief against corporation tax on the interest.

Again because the cost of this form of instalment finance varies considerably from one finance house to another it is prudent to shop around to find the most advantageous terms. It is important to know and compare the true rate of interest quoted by each finance house approached.

4.21 Factoring

One of the main problems faced by small companies is the difficulty of getting customers, especially larger companies, to pay their bills on time. One of the ways to speed up the flow of cash from credit sales is to make use of the facility known as factoring. Factoring is basically an arrangement to sell trade debts in order to raise finance.

There are several forms of factoring including the 'normal' factoring service, confidential factoring and invoice discounting. Under the normal service the factor discounts outstanding invoices by advancing up to 80 per cent of the face value within predetermined credit limits set by the factor for each debtor. This system also includes a complete sales ledger, debt collection and accounting service by the factor and may include protection against bad debts. It is suitable for a company which is expanding rapidly and has a good spread of creditworthy debtors. A charge of between 1 and 3 per cent of factoring turnover is made to cover the bookkeeping service and credit protection and the discounting finance costs between 2 and 5 per cent, above base rate.

The system for confidential factoring is similar to normal factoring but the client has his own sales ledger and is responsible for collecting the debts. This has the advantage that the debtors do not know of the factor's involvement. The client submits copy invoices to the factor periodically and receives the advance. He receives payments from the debtor 'in trust' for the factor to whom he must pay back any amount originally advanced on that debt.

Where a company has a small number of invoices made out to companies of good repute for relatively large amounts invoice discounting may be considered. In this case up to 75 per cent of invoice value may be advanced but the client has the responsibility of debt collection and onward transmission of the funds to settle the advances from the discounting company. Any accounts over-due beyond the normal date of payment, in the trade, must be funded by the client not the factor to the eventual date of payment. Bad debt cover is not normally available and the costs range between 0.25 and 0.75 of a per cent of the turnover plus charges which are between 2 and 5 per cent above base rate.

The main trade association is the Association of British Factors which has eight members. Turnover in 1984 by the members of the association was £3.8 billion which indicates that factoring is now both an acceptable and accepted form of finance.

Factoring is basically a source of short-term finance, easing cash flow and increasing working capital but it should not be used to provide funds for the purchase of assets. Factoring is not really open to a company just starting up, but once it is trading factoring can help to accelerate its growth.

4.22 Self-Financing

Before completing this section of the book on finance it is impor-tant to state the obvious. The organization of a company's own financial affairs by proper management and financial controls and the use of its own resources is the cheapest source from which a company can obtain funds. The early collection of trade debts while taking the full credit terms allowed by suppliers will improve cash flow. It is important to monitor the company's cash flow to minimize interest charges but not to the extent that the company's future is endangered by lack of adequate working capital.

4.23 Insurance

By forming a private limited company the reader will have effected the cheapest and possibly the best business insurance available. In fact it is probably the only insurance available to the entrepreneur which protects him from loss of his personal assets and property should his business fail.

This having been said it is prudent for the company to take out insurances against the different misfortunes which the business may meet in the course of trading. Insurance is important and adequacy of cover against insurable risks cannot be over-emphasized.

Insurance has to be considered from two angles:

(a) Voluntary insurance.
(b) Compulsory insurance required by law.

Before dealing with details of insurance policies available a word of advice on insurance brokers. 'Insurance broker' is an expression, the use of which is limited, to persons, firms or companies which have been accepted for registration by the Insurance Brokers Registration Council under the Insurance Brokers (Registration) Act 1977.

The trade body representing registered insurance brokers is the British Insurance Brokers Association (BIBA) who maintain a list of members. Not all persons, firms or companies selling insurance are members. Accordingly, it is recommended that advice is sought only from members of BIBA.

Insurance Brokers do not charge for the advice they give. Their income is derived from the commission they are paid by insurance companies on the policies issued. If the insurance broker is presented with full details of the company's business, assets and staff he will be able to recommend the various types of insurance available. In addition he will be able to obtain the keenest quotations for the different policies suggested.

Almost any risk can be insured against, and the principal insurances effected by a business concern will depend upon the nature of the business. Most businesses insure against fire, accident, burglary and similar risks to which almost any establishment is vulnerable. In a manufacturing concern, the factory buildings would normally be insured against loss by fire, flood, frost, burst pipes and boilers, etc. Machinery, equipment, plant, boilers, air compressors and electrical equipment would be insured against risk of fire or breakdown. Stock-in-trade would be covered against loss by fire, water damage or burglary. A shop would additionally require cover for plate glass. Business premises which have a lift would insure against loss resulting from breakdown of the lift.

A great deal of insurance business is done and the reason for this is not far to seek. Protections can be obtained against many risks by payment of annual premiums of comparatively small amounts to insurers and underwriters, who, in relieving the trader of their risks, rely upon the probability that only a relatively small number of losses will, in fact, be incurred so that the large number of premiums received will normally be more than sufficient to satisfy the claims made by persons who suffer loss, and leave a profit for the insurer.

Where the insurance is against the loss of a business asset by any cause it is wise to check that the sum insured is index-linked and the value of the insured item is adjusted at regular intervals. This type of policy is sometimes referred to as 'new for old'.

Traders Combined Policies

To simplify insurance cover most insurance companies issue an 'all in' policy which is suitable for a factory, an office or a shop. This will include cover against risks including fire, flood and other natural hazards and loss of goods and the damage to property caused by burglary. In addition to this type of policy there are

75

other voluntary insurance policies which should be considered. It is not unusual to find these included in the traders combined policy.

Fidelity Insurance
Under this policy the insurer undertakes to make good loss caused by dishonesty of persons through whose hands pass large sums of money belonging to the insured.

Consequential Loss and Loss of Profits
Where the business of the company has been interrupted by a fire or other cause there may be expenses that cannot be terminated immediately if the business stops, and those which do not diminish proportionately to lower sales during partial interruption. This type of policy provides indemnity against the trading loss so arising. Where a company suffers a complete loss of business following a fire there will be both a loss of continuing expenses and of profits which if uninsured might result in the collapse of the company.

Cash in Transit
If it is the practice to carry or to allow staff to carry cash to and from the bank (e.g. takings and staff wages) a policy can be taken out to cover any losses incurred during the journey.

Professional Negligence
This will normally apply to a service industry where advice given by the company is acted upon and results in a claim for losses or damage. Accountants and solicitors are invariably insured against this risk but there are many other service industries where this cover is essential. It is not unknown for prospective customers to enquire whether a policy exists before placing business with the company offering the service.

Bad Debts
In the section on factoring earlier in this part of the book, it was mentioned that the factor may include protection against bad debts in the normal factoring service. This protection is available through insurance, but the insured will be required to keep his debtor

records in a fire-proof safe. Insurance is also available where debtors' records are destroyed in a fire resulting in the loss of those debts. The insurance company will normally require duplicate records to be kept and for at least one set to be kept in a fireproof container.

Vehicle Insurance

In addition to the compulsory third party claims insurance required by law it is prudent to consider comprehensive cover against loss by theft of, and the cost of damage to, the company's vehicles. If goods are carried in the company's vehicles insurance should be taken out to compensate for loss of goods in transit.

Keyman Insurance

The man or woman whose death could mean financial problems to the company can be the subject of an insurance policy. The loss of certain key personnel can be as damaging to a business as any of the other insurable risks. However the number of companies which are covered for this possibility is very small. This important protection is very popular in America.

Export Credit Guarantees

For companies in the export business the Exports Credits Guarantee Department (ECGD) can help in two ways: It can insure them against the risks of not being paid for their exports and may be able to give a guarantee to their bank under which finance can be obtained for export business. ECGD is a government department which will cover the exporter for 90 per cent of his losses if the foreign buyer fails to pay for the goods exported.

Public Liability Insurance

The object of a public liability policy is to protect the insured against his legal liability for bodily injury to third parties (not employees) or loss of or damage to their property where such injury or damage occurs on or near the premises of the insured. The public liability policy does not cover the insured's legal liability arising from every cause and some may be covered under other policies, e.g. engineering policies may cover public liability risks associated with boilers or passenger lifts. Not all public liability insurance is compulsory.

Employers' Liability Insurance
This compulsory insurance is regulated by the Employers' Liability (Compulsory Insurance) Act 1969. All employers must cover against liability for bodily injury and disease sustained by their employees, arising out of their employment. The amount for which an employer is required by the act to insure and maintain insurance is £2,000,000 in respect of claims relating to any one or more of his employees arising out of any one occurrence. A copy or copies of the certificate of insurance issued by the insurance company have to be displayed at each place of business where employees work.

National Insurance
Employers are required by law to pay a national insurance contribution for each employee. The employer is also responsible for deducting the employee's national insurance contribution from wages and salaries paid to him and to pay these to the Inland Revenue with the PAYE deductions. For employers who have not contracted out of the State scheme, the contributions are on a graduated scale so that people on low earnings and their employers pay lower contributions. From 6 October 1985 for employees earning below £35.50 per week there will be no liability for employee or employer. The employee does not pay contributions on earnings exceeding £265 per week but for employers the contribution will be 10.45% of all earnings with no upper limit.

APPENDICES

Appendix I

Notes for Guidance on Company Names

Appendix IA

The following words and expressions will require the consent of the Secretary of State for Trade before their use will be allowed in a company name. The words fall into the following categories:

Guidance notes on the sensitive words and expressions outlined in Appendix IA are available from the Companies Registration Office in a small booklet entitled *Company and Business Names: Notes on Sensitive Words and Expressions* (Ref. C499, March 1985).

(a) Words which imply national or international pre-eminence.

International	Scotland
National	Scottish
European	Wales
United Kingdom	Welsh
Great Britain	Ireland
British	Irish
England	
English	

(b) Words which imply govermental patronage or sponsorship.

Authority
Board
Council

(c) Words which imply business pre-eminence or representative status.

Association
Federation

Society
Institute
Institution

(d) Words which imply specific objects or functions.

Assurance	Group
Assurer	Holdings
Reassurance	
Reassurer	Stock Exchange
	Register
Insurance	Registered
Insurer	
Reinsurance	Friendly Society
Reinsurer	Industrial and Provident Society
Patent	
Patentee	Building Society
	Trade Union
Chamber of Commerce	Foundation
Chamber of Trade	Fund
Chamber of Industry	Charter
Co-operative	Chartered
	Sheffield
Chemist	Benevolent
Chemistry	

Post Office
Giro
Trust

Appendix IB

The following words and expressions also require the Secretary of State's consent and normally a company would be registered by a name containing any of the following words or expressions only if the applicant had obtained a letter of non-objection from the relevant Department or Body. Any correspondence should be submitted with the appropriate registration documents.

Word or Expression	Relevant Body for Companies Intending to Have Registered Office in England or Wales	Relevant Body for Companies Intending to Have Registered Office in Scotland
Royal, Royale, Royalty, King, Queen, Prince Princess, Windsor, Duke, His/Her Majesty	Miss N D Marks E2 Division (Room 820) Home Office Queen Anne's Gate London SW1H 9AT	Miss Bell Scottish Home and Health Department Old St Andrews House Edinburgh EH1 3DE
Police	Mr F Osmond F1 Division Police Department Home Office Queen Anne's Gate London SW1H 9AT	Mr Samuels Police Division Old St Andrews House Edinburgh EH1 3DE
Special School	Mrs P A Masters Schools II Branch Department of Education and Science Elizabeth House York Road London SE1 7PH	As for England and Wales

Contact Lens	The Registrar General Optical Council 41 Harley Street London W1N 2DJ	As for England and Wales
Dental, Dentistry	The Registrar General Dental Council 37 Wimpole Street London W1M 8DQ	As for England and Wales
Nurse, Nursing, Midwife, Midwifery, Health Visitor	Chief Executive Officer United Kingdom Central Council for Nursing Midwifery and Health Visiting 23 Portland Place London W1A 1BA	As for England and Wales
District Nurse	Panel of Assessors in District Nurse Training Room 706 Hannibal House Elephant and Castle London SE1 6TE	As for England and Wales
Health Centre	Division PP1A (Room C206) Department of Health and Social Security Alexander Fleming House Elephant and Castle London SE1 6TE	As for England and Wales

| Health Service | HS2D Division
Department of Health
and Social Security
Hannibal House
Elephant and Castle
London SE1 6TE | As for England and
Wales |

Appendix IC

The use of certain words in company names is covered by other legislation and their unauthorized use may constitute a criminal offence. Some of these words are listed below, but the list is not exhaustive. Companies wishing to use any of these words in their name should seek confirmation from either the relevant body listed or from the Companies Registration Offices that the use of the word in a company name does not contravene the relevant legislation.

Word or Expression	Relevant Legislation	Relevant Body
Architect, Architectural	Section 1, Architects Registration Act 1938	The Registrar Architects Registration Council of the United Kingdom 73 Hallam Street London W1N 6EE
Credit Union	Credit Union Act 1979	Registry of Friendly Societies 15/17 Great Marlborough Street London W1V 2AX

Veterinary Surgeon	Sections 19 and 20, Veterinary Surgeons Act 1966	The Registrar Royal College of Veterinary Surgeons 32 Belgrave Square London SW1X 8QP
Dentist, Dental Surgeon, Dental Practitioner	Sections 38 and 39, Dentist Act 1957	The Registrar General Dental Council 37 Wimpole Street London W1M 8DQ
Drug, Druggist, Pharmaceutical, Pharmaceutist, Pharmacist, Pharmacy	Section 78, Medicines Act 1968	Seek advice of Companies Registration Office (CRO)
Ophthalmic Optician, Dispensing Optician, Registered Optician	Sections 4 and 22, Opticians Act 1958	The Registrar General Optical Council 41 Harley Street London W1N 2D5
Bank, Banker, Banking Deposit	Banking Act 1979	Bank of England Threadneedle Street London EC2R 8AM
Red Cross	Geneva Convention Act 1957	Seek Advice of CRO
Anzac	Section 1, Anzac Act 1916	Seek Advice of CRO

Insurance Broker	Sections 2 and 3,	Seek Advice of CRO
Assurance Broker	Insurance Brokers	
Reinsurance	(Registration) Act	
Broker		
Reassurance		
Broker		

Appendix ID

'Too Like' Names

In considering whether names are 'too like', the Secretary of State must be prepared to take account of all factors which may be considered to suggest similarity and lead to confusion between the names of two companies. These will include, for example, the nature and location of the businesses concerned.

Subject to this requirement names may be considered to be 'too like' in the opinion of the Secretary of State:

(a) If the names are phonetically identical.

(b) If there is only a slight variation in the spelling of the two names and the variation does not make a significant difference between the names.

(c) If in the case of an oversea company registered under Part X of the Companies Act 1948, the names differ from a name already on the index only by the substitution of the oversea country equivalent of *Limited, Unlimited* or *Public Limited Company.*

(d) If the names contain a word or words which might be regarded as a distinctive element, unless that element is qualified in such a way as would minimize risk of confusion. A distinctive element will normally be defined as 'made up words', 'non-dictionary words' or 'combinations of 2 or more letters as a prefix'. In some cases everyday words used in a 'distinctive' way may also be considered as distinctive elements. Place names or everyday descriptive words in general use will not normally be regarded as distinctive. Similar descriptive elements, e.g. press/printing, staff agency/employment agency, or the inclusion in one name of only a general or 'weak' qualification such as holding, group, system, services, etc., would not normally be regarded as a sufficient qualification.

Examples

(a) Names which are the same — Mayfair Engineering Limited v Mayfair Engineering Company, Limited.
(b) Names which are phonetically identical — Lyfestyle Limited v Lifestyle Limited and AB-Chem Limited v Abkem Limited.
(c) Names in which the slight variation in spelling does not make a significant difference Consolair Ltd v Consulair Ltd.
(d) Names which contain the same distinctive element:
  (i) Where the names are sufficiently qualified — Factromatic Computers Limited v Factromatic Plant Hire Limited.
  (ii) Where the names are not sufficiently qualified — Mechala Limited v Mechala Holding Limited or Oddbods Press Limited v Oddbods Printing Limited.
(e) Names which are 'Like' where other factors may be relevant — Plan Travel Limited v Planned Travel Limited.

Appendix II

Company Formation Forms: Prescribed Forms, Memorandum and Articles of Association

The forms in this appendix are those prescribed by the Companies (Forms) Regulations 1985 for use when registering a limited company.

For the purposes of this appendix we are forming a hypothetical company:

Jordans Private Company Limited

with two promoters/subscribers who will each take one share. They are David John Grant and John Regan, the former will be the sole director of the company and the latter will be secretary.

COMPANIES FORM No. 10

Statement of first directors and secretary and intended situation of registered office

Pursuant to section 10 of the Companies Act 1985

To the Registrar of Companies

For official use

Name of company

*   JORDANS PRIVATE COMPANY LIMITED

The intended situation of the registered office of the company on incorporation is as stated below

15 PEMBROKE ROAD		
CLIFTON		
BRISTOL		
	Postcode	BS8 3BA

If the memorandum is delivered by an agent for the subscribers of the memorandum please mark 'X' in the box opposite and insert the agent's name and address below

[X]

JORDAN & SONS LIMITED		
15 PEMBROKE ROAD		
CLIFTON		
BRISTOL	Postcode	BS8 3BA

Number of continuation sheets attached (see note 1) [ ]

PRINTED AND SUPPLIED BY

Jordans

JORDAN & SONS LIMITED
JORDAN HOUSE
BRUNSWICK PLACE
LONDON N1 6EE
TELEPHONE 01 253 3030
TELEX 261010

Presentor's name address and reference (if any):

For official Use	
General Section	Post room

Page 1

90

The name(s) and particulars of the person who is, or the persons who are, to be the first director or directors of the company (note 2) are as follows:

Name (note 3)	Business occupation
DAVID JOHN GRANT	Company Formation Assistant
Previous name(s) (note 3) NONE	Nationality
Address (note 4) 15 PEMBROKE ROAD	British
CLIFTON	Date of birth (where applicable)
BRISTOL Postcode BS8 3BA	(note 6)

Other directorships †

† enter particulars of other directorships held or previously held (see note 5) if this space is insufficient use a continuation sheet.

I consent to act as director of the company named on page 1

Signature   D J Grant   Date   22 January 1986

Name (note 3)	Business occupation
Previous name(s) (note 3)	Nationality
Address (note 4)	
	Date of birth (where applicable)
Postcode	(note 6)

Other directorships †

I consent to act as director of the company named on page 1

Signature   Date

Name (note 3)	Business occupation
Previous name(s) (note 3)	Nationality
Address (note 4)	
	Date of birth (where applicable)
Postcode	(note 6)

Other directorships †

I consent to act as director of the company named on page 1

Signature   Date

The name(s) and particulars of the person who is, or the persons who are, to be the first secretary, or joint secretaries, of the company are as follows:

Name (notes 3 & 7)		
JOHN REGAN		
Previous name(s) (note 3) NONE		
Address (notes 4 & 7) 15 PEMBROKE ROAD		
CLIFTON		
BRISTOL	Postcode	BS8 3BA

I consent to act as secretary of the company named on page 1

Signature *John Regan*   Date   22 January 1986

Name (notes 3 & 7)		
Previous name(s) (note 3)		
Address (notes 4 & 7)		
	Postcode	

I consent to act as secretary of the company named on page 1

Signature   Date

Signature of agent on behalf of subsribers   Date 22.1.86

delete if the form is signed by an agent on behalf of the subscribers.

All the subscribers must sign either personally or by a person or persons authorised to sign for them.

Signed	Date
Signed	Date
Signed	Date
Signed	Date
Signed	Date
Signed	Date

Page 3

92

Form No. PUC1 (revised)

G

Statement on formation of a company to be incorporated with limited liability under the Companies Act 1985

Pursuant to Part V of the Finance Act 1973

PUC1

Please do not write in this binding margin

Please complete legibly, preferably in black type, or bold block lettering

*delete if inappropriate

†Distinguish between ordinary, preference, etc.

For official use

Company number

Please do not write in the space below. For Inland Revenue use only

Name of company

JORDANS PRIVATE COMPANY LIMITED

Limited*

A Nominal Capital		£	
Description of shares†			Ordinary
B Nominal value of each share	£	£	£ 1
C Number of shares taken on incorporation			TWO
D Total amount payable on each (including premium if any)	£	£	£ NIL*
E Amount paid or due and payable on each	£	£	£ NIL
F Total amount paid or due and payable in respect of C		£ NIL	
G Capital duty payable on F at £1 per £100 or part of £100		£ NIL	

Notes

This form must be delivered to the Registrar of Companies when applying for incorporation of the company.

If amounts are contributed otherwise than in cash, that fact with full particulars must be stated and attached to this form

Please tick box if attached

I hereby certify that the above particulars are correct in all respects

:delete as appropriate

Signed _D J Gant_ [Director] [Secretary]‡ Date 22/1/86

Presentor's name, address and reference (if any):

For official use

Capital section

Post room

PRINTED AND SUPPLIED BY
Jordans
JORDAN & SONS LIMITED
JORDAN HOUSE
BRUNSWICK PLACE
LONDON N1 6EE
TELEPHONE 01-253 3030
TELEX 261010

* By issuing the subscribers' shares as 'Nil Paid' it is possible to avoid possible stamping delays.

G

COMPANIES FORM No. 12

Statutory Declaration of compliance with requirements on application for registration of a company

12

Please do not write in this margin

Pursuant to section 12(3) of the Companies Act 1985

Please complete legibly, preferably in black type, or bold block lettering

To the Registrar of Companies

For official use

For official use

Name of company

* insert full name of Company

* JORDANS PRIVATE COMPANY LIMITED

I, JOHN REGAN

of 15 PEMBROKE ROAD

CLIFTON

BRISTOL BS8 3BA

† delete as appropriate

do solemnly and sincerely declare that I am a [Solicitor engaged in the formation of the company]†
[person named as director or secretary of the company in the statement delivered to the registrar
under section 10(2)]† and that all the requirements of the above Act in respect of the registration of the
above company and of matters precedent and incidental to it have been complied with,

And I make this solemn declaration conscientiously believing the same to be true and by virtue of the
provisions of the Statutory Declarations Act 1835

Declared at 15 PEMBROKE ROAD

CLIFTON

BRISTOL BS8 3BA

the 22nd day of January

One thousand nine hundred and eighty six

before me Roger Martin

A Commissioner for Oaths or Notary Public or Justice of
the Peace or Solicitor having the powers conferred on a
Commissioner for Oaths.

Declarant to sign below

John Regan

PRINTED AND SUPPLIED BY

Jordans

JORDAN & SONS LIMITED
JORDAN HOUSE
BRUNSWICK PLACE
LONDON N1 6EE
TELEPHONE 01 253 3030
TELEX 261010

Presentor's name address and
reference (if any):

For official Use

New Companies Section

Post room

94

Subscriber's page to the memorandum of association

WE, the subscribers to this Memorandum of Association wish to be formed into a Company pursuant to this Memorandum; and we agree to take the number of shares shown opposite out respective names.

Names and Addresses of Subcribers	Number of shares taken by each subscriber
1. David John Grant 15 Pembroke Road Clifton Bristol BS8 3BA *D J Grant*	— One
2. John Regan 15 Pembroke Road Clifton Bristol BS8 3BA *John Regan*	— One
Total shares taken	— Two

Dated 22 January 1986

Witness to the above Signatures: Errol Sandiford
15 Pembroke road
Bristol BS8 3BA

95

Subscribers' page to the articles of association

Names and addresses of Subscribers

1.   David John Grant
     15 Pembroke Road
     Clifton
     Bristol BS8 3BA

     DJ Grant

2.   John Regan
     15 Pembroke Road
     Clifton
     Bristol BS8 3BA

     John Regan

Dated 22 January 1986

Witness to the above Signatures: Errol Sandiford
                                   15 Pembroke Road
                                   Bristol BS8 3BA

Appendix III

Useful Addresses and/or Telephone Numbers

ACAS
Head Office
11–12 St. James's Square
London SW1Y 4LA
Tel. 01 214 6000

Association of British Factors
Hind Court
147 Fleet Street
London EC4A 2BU
Tel. 01 353 1213

Association of Certified Accountants
29 Lincolns Inn Fields
London WC2A 3AA
Tel. 01 242 6855

Association of Company Registration Agents
Temple House
20 Holywell Row
London EC2A 4JB
Tel. 01 377 0381

British Insurance Brokers Association
Biba House
14 Bevis Marks
London EC3A 7NT
Tel. 01 623 9043

Business Expansion Scheme Funds
   Centreway BES
   Tel. 021 643 3941

   Charterhouse BE Funds
   Tel. 01 247 4000

   Electra Risk Capital
   Tel. 01 836 7766

   Guidehouse ES
   Tel. 01 606 6321

   London Venture Capital Market Ltd
   Tel. 01 629 5983

   Northern Venture Capital
   Tel. 031 557 3560

Business in the Community
(for Local Enterprise Agencies)
91 Waterloo Road
London SE1 8XP
Tel. 01 928 6423

Company Formation Agents
   Jordan & Sons Ltd
   15 Pembroke Road
   Bristol BS8 3BA
   Tel. 0272 732861

   Jordan & Sons Ltd
   Jordan House
   Brunswick Place
   London N1 6EE
   Tel. 01 253 3030

Jordan & Sons Ltd
3rd Floor
21 Bennetts Hill
Birmingham B2 5QP
Tel. 021 632 6633

Jordan & Sons Ltd
44 Whitchurch Road
Cardiff CF4 3UQ
Tel. 0222 371901

Oswalds of Edinburgh Ltd
24 Castle Street
Edinburgh EH2 3HT
Tel. 031 225 7308

Jordan & Sons (Isle of Man) Ltd
Victory House
Prospect Hill
Douglas
Isle of Man
Tel. 0624 24298

Jordan & Sons Ltd
11 York Place
Leeds LS1 2DS
Tel. 0532 436116

Jordan & Sons Ltd
3 Victoria Street
Liverpool L2 5QF
Tel. 051 236 4564

Jordan & Sons Ltd
47 Mosley Street
Manchester M60 8AA
Tel. 061 236 0309

Jordan & Sons Ltd
Exchange Buildings
Quayside
Newcastle Upon Tyne NE1 3AQ
Tel. 0632 329394

Express Company Registrations Ltd
Epworth House
25-35 City Road
London EC1Y 1AA
Tel. 01 588 3271

Hart & Co. Ltd
47 Brunswick Place
London N1 6EE
Tel. 01 250 1841

Council for Small Industries in Rural Areas (CoSIRA)
Head Office
141 Castle Street
Salisbury SP1 3TP
Tel. 0722 6255

Customs and Excise, HM
  VAT Central Unit
  Alexander House
  21 Victoria Avenue
  Southend on Sea SS99 1AB

  VAT London Head Office
  Northgate House
  1 Remnant Street
  Lincolns Inn Fields
  London WC2A 3JH
  Tel. 01 405 8777

Department of Trade and Industry Regional Offices and
Department of Trade — Support for Business Information Service
Tel. 01 215 4021

North East
Tel. 0632 324 722

North West
Tel. 061 236 2171

Yorkshire and Humberside
Tel. 0532 443 171

East Midlands
Tel. 0602 506 181

West Midlands
Tel. 021 632 4111

South East
Tel. 01 730 9678

South West
Tel. 0272 272 666

Scotland
Tel. 041 248 2855

Wales
Tel. 0222 825 111

Northern Ireland
Tel. 0232 233 233

Department of Trade Small Firms Service
Ebury Bridge House
2–18 Ebury Bridge Road
London SW1W 8QD
Tel. Freefone 2444

Equipment Leasing Association
18 Upper Grosvenor Street
London W1X 9PB
Tel. 01 491 2783

Exports Credits Guarantee Department
Head Office
PO Box 272
Aldermanbury House
London EC2P 2EL
Tel. 01 382 7000

Inspector of Taxes, HM
Head Office Enquiries
Somerset House
London WC2R 1LB
Tel. 01 438 6420

Institute of Chartered Accountants in England and Wales
399 Silbury Boulevard
Wigan Gate East
Central Milton Keynes MK9 2HL
Tel. 01 628 7060

Institute of Chartered Secretaries and Administrators
16 Park Crescent
London W1N 4AH
Tel. 01 580 4741

Insurance Brokers Registration Council
15 St Helens Place

London EC3
Tel. 01 588 4387

Investors in Industry Group Plc
91 Waterloo Road
London SE1 8XP
Tel. 01 928 7822

Law Society, The
113 Chancery Lane
London WC2A 1PL
Tel. 01 242 1222

Loan Guarantee Scheme
(see Department of Trade Support for Business Information
   Service)

Registrar of Companies, The
Companies Registration Office
Crown Way
Maindy
Cardiff CF4 3UZ
Tel. 0222 388 588

Registrar of Companies, The
Companies Registration Office
102 George Street
Edinburgh EH2 3DJ
Tel. 031 255 5774

Registrar of Companies, The
Companies Registry
43/47 Chichester Street
Belfast BT1 4RJ
Northern Ireland
Tel. Belfast 34121/4

Trade Marks Registry, The
69/71 State House
High Holborn
London WC1R 4SX
Tel. 01 405 8721

Index

107